DATE DUE

Stone Style

Stone Style

Michael Reis and
Jennifer Adams

Gibbs Smith, Publisher
Salt Lake City

First Edition

06 05 04 03 02   5 4 3 2 1

Published by

Gibbs Smith, Publisher

P.O. Box 667

Layton, Utah 84041

Orders: (1-800) 748-5439

www.gibbs-smith.com

Designed by Kurt Wahlner

Edited by Madge Baird

Printed in Hong Kong

Half-title page, photograph by Kurt Wahlner, © Gibbs Smith, Publisher

Facing title page, photograph by Don Pearse Photographers Inc.

Library of Congress Cataloging-in-Publication Data

Reis, Michael.

    Stone style : by Michael Reis and Jennifer Adams.—1st ed.

      p. cm.

   ISBN 1-58685-117-9

1. Architecture, Domestic—United States. 2. Stone buildings—United

States. 3. Stone in interior decoration. 4. Architecture—United

States—20th century. I. Adams, Jennifer. II. Title.

   NA7208 .R44 2002

   728'.37'0973—dc21

                    2001005140

Contents

Introduction

In stark contrast to European preferences—where stone has traditionally been part and parcel of residential design—the North American trend in homebuilding has historically been defined by man-made materials such as aluminum siding, carpeting and linoleum. And while natural stone has not been completely absent from American homebuilding over the past two centuries, it has generally been a material considered only for the highest end of the building spectrum.

However, consumer awareness about natural stone has increased over the past few decades, and with this has come a broadening of the design palette. Natural stone is finding its way into design plans for everyday residences, as homeowners are taking notice of not only the aesthetic benefits but also the practical advantages of the material. Using natural stone in residential design opens the door to endless possibilities. With such a wide range of materials on the market today, just about any look imaginable can be created.

For architect Kevin McKenna of Kevin McKenna Architects in Columbia, Maryland, each custom-home design he works on can differ drastically from client to client. But one common thread that seems to be evident is the role natural stone plays in its development.

Conceiving a residential scheme that is specifically designed for a homeowner is not only an aesthetic challenge but also often involves educating a client. "Custom homes are always difficult," he said. "Usually, it is the first time that they have done something like this. Many folks have trouble understanding that it is custom work, and therefore it may take more time."

McKenna went on to explain that he meets two categories of people. "There are 'blank page' people who don't know what they want, and there are 'rigid thinking' people

With multiple rooflines echoing the Rocky Mountains in the background, the design and materials of the Paul and Kay Stephan home in Alpine, Utah, has the rustic look the Stephans wanted. The native stone is locally referred to as East Desert Rock. The chimney was designed on the spot by the masons, who took advantage of the stone to create an inverted bell shape.

Architect: **Gordon Jacobson**
Builder: **L & T Construction, Orem, Utah**
Stonemason: **Brent Miller, Orem, Utah**
Stone Supplier: **Jensen Stone, Talmage, Utah**
Photo: **Kurt Wahlner**

who know what they want and don't want to look at alternatives," he said. "I try to find a common ground and work through the issues. It's certainly not fair for me to disregard the ideas that they have had their entire life."

But one thing is certain, "Almost everyone—regardless of their taste—will have an interest in stone," said McKenna. "It's one of the root materials in terms of available products." Of course, budgets come into play when deciding how much stone will actually be used for a home. "We try to always give people a touch of stone," he said. "But I can't force them to spend the money to put stone on the entire building."

One important point McKenna stresses is that natural stone should be used appropriately. "When stone is a desired item, but budget limits our ability to do it right, what I try to do is limit the amount," he said. "I'd rather use less stone and use it appropriately."

Learning about finishes

Numerous surface finishes—which are administered at the time of fabrication and include polished, honed, sandblasted, tumbled, bushhammered, and flamed—also play an important role in achieving the desired effect of a design. The consideration in choosing a proper finish is just as critical as selecting the stone itself. Each finish possesses its own unique characteristics and can drastically change the appearance of a stone.

Polished materials have been treated with abrasives of gradually increasing grits until a shiny, high-gloss look is achieved. They set the stage for an elegant foyer or a formal dining or living space. Additionally, a polished granite countertop can provide a clean, contemporary look in most kitchens.

In contrast, honed stone finishes are more subdued and conservative. The surfaces of these stones have also been treated with abrasives, but to a lesser grit than polished stone. Materials with these finishes typically evoke a welcoming and comfortable atmosphere. Expanding on this concept, stone fabricators are also producing tumbled-stone finishes, which are produced by loading stone tiles into a heavy barrel tumbler filled with water and abrasives and literally tumbling the tiles for a predetermined amount of time. The result is stone tile with a patina

that appears to have been created by years of foot traffic and natural wear.

For a more rustic approach to residential design, a bushhammered or sand-blasted finish would be an appropriate choice. These finishes provide a rough-textured look and feel to stone. They can be achieved with either high-tech machinery, which automatically furnishes the desired look of stone, or with hand tools, where skilled workers create the finish by hand. Since these finishes are more slip-resistant than polished material, they are appropriate for applications such as stairs or high-traffic floor areas.

Tumbled marble was employed to conjure an old-world feel in this residence. Various patterns were made with the material to create diversity in the design. Extending the use of the tumbled stone from the hallway to the bathroom portrays a continuous theme throughout the home.

Designer: **Calder Interiors, New York, New York** • *Photo:* **Phillip H. Ennis**

The floor in this spacious residence features 16 x 16-inch Durango Classic stone tiles with a honed and filled finish. The light color and large format of the tiles, combined with the floor-to-ceiling windows, assist in creating an open, airy feel to the room.

Determining a style

The stone selection process can be overwhelming if homeowners are undecided on the residential style they prefer. Just like finishes, different types of natural stone lend themselves to specific looks.

For example, a honed limestone or travertine floor can conjure a warm inviting feeling in a living space, while polished marble tiles can seem more formal. If homeowners envision a residence where they can entertain their family and guests

Stone Supplier:
World Wide Stone Corp.,
Phoenix, Arizona

Using a honed or tumbled limestone on the exterior of a residence can also achieve an old-world style. Large-format stone pieces are also ideal for driveway and walkway paving.

Stone Supplier: **Walker Zanger, Sylmar, California**

In this kitchen, Indian Tropical Green granite-slab countertops complement wooden cabinetry. The detailed edges and rich color add to the elegance of the room.

Designer: **Naomi Reese, Dallas, Texas**
Stone Supplier: **Stone-Tec, Garland, Texas**

in a friendly relaxed setting, then a "softer" stone might be a more suitable option. On the other hand, if they picture themselves living in a lavish home that makes a grand statement to their guests, marble or granite would be the way to go.

For nature lovers who desire a home that reflects a rustic outdoor environment, slate and fieldstone are ideal materials. Floor-to-ceiling fieldstone fireplaces can make a residential living space feel just like the interior of a mountain cabin or ski lodge. Many people also use fieldstone on exterior façades to create the appearance of an old farmhouse. A common trend is also to employ fieldstone on additional walls throughout the interior of the home to continue that aged look.

Slate—with its natural cleft texture—can also provide a rustic style. Commonly used as flooring, the material is also well suited for walls and tub surrounds. Outside the home, slate is a practical, aesthetically pleasing choice for walkways, patios and roofing.

Natural stone can also achieve a contemporary feel. Usually kept to a simple color palette, these designs incorporate polished granites and marbles to present a

sleek modern look. Although not as warm as the casual atmosphere created with muted limestone or travertine, the contemporary style does not have an intimidating air. It is a trim look that does not include the ornate detailing found in more elaborate residences that use polished stone.

Selecting a color palette

In addition to the abundance of material options that are available, color scheme also needs to be taken into consideration. When going through the selection process, homeowners will discover that each type of stone—including marble, granite, slate, limestone, travertine and sandstone—is offered in an array of colors.

Although color selection is not limited to the style of the residence, certain colors are more appropriate for specific designs. New quarries are continually being opened all around the world, and homeowners will find that there are shades available to meet every desired color palette.

A casual European style was chosen by homeowners Bruce and Edna Albertson. For a bit of an old-world feel to correlate with the outside of their home (see p. 19), the Albertsons selected a backsplash and range hood faced with diagonally laid tumbled travertine tiles. The bas relief inset panel adds interest that lifts this kitchen out of the ordinary.

Designer/General Contractor:
   Cameo Homes,
   Sandy, Utah
Stonemason:
   James Routi,
   Bountiful, Utah
Stone Supplier:
   Contempo Tile,
   Salt Lake City, Utah
Photo:
   Kurt Wahlner

13

Exotic stones imported from South America and India feature vibrant hues such as yellow, green, and purple. In contrast, mild shades of beige and cream stones—usually extracted from quarries in Europe—are available for the conservative homeowner. While both types of stones might seem appealing, homeowners need to consider the look they are trying to achieve. If the theme of a home is an old-world style—complete with tumbled limestone walls and floors—a brightly colored polished marble might not be a practical choice for a vanity top. In the same respect, a fieldstone fireplace surround might not be the best complement to a polished marble floor.

There are ways, however, to incorporate various stones into a design as accent materials. For example, in a kitchen that is mostly comprised of shades of beige and cream, color can be added by including a mosaic backsplash or a border in the floor. The same can be true for a powder room. Additionally, mosaic inlays can spice up the appearance of a foyer floor.

Developing a relationship

To avoid any miscommunication, McKenna stresses the importance for homeowners to build close relationships with their architects or designers. "When I work well with a client on a custom home, I really get to know them," he said. "Nothing I do is pre-drawn. We work together for a long time."

For one project, McKenna worked with a couple who were open to many creative possibilities. "They were willing to take more chances than any client I've ever had," he said. "They had expressed interest in some antique buildings that they had seen in various travels. The stone and mortar in those buildings had deteriorated, and that was the look we were trying to accomplish. We left stone visible at the foundation, and the detached garage had exposed stone at the foundation level."

McKenna went on to explain that although the entire home was new construction, the idea of the design was to make it appear as if an addition was made to an old stone house. "What we tried to do there was build a home that mimicked the way homes were in the early periods, and then we added modern elements. It mimicked an old stone house that was stuccoed over."

Opposite:

For most features of the home, the Walkers relied on their designer/builder's expertise. But they had a unique idea for the entryway that the builder was happy to execute: a diagonal gridwork of cherry wood inlaid with slate. The result creates a stunning first impression.

Designer/General Contractor:
**Cameo Homes,
Sandy, Utah**
Photo:
Kurt Wahlner

Natural stone is also a great way to enhance a sunroom or closed-in porch. For this application, Fontenay Claire honed limestone in 16 x 16-inch tiles, with 2 x 2-inch Heliodoro limestone accents, which were used for the flooring. Cladding the base of the wall with fieldstone further evokes the rustic feel.

Stone Supplier:
**Walker Zanger,
Sylmar, California**
Installer:
**Country Flair Tile,
Kent, Connecticut**

Practical considerations for specifying natural stone

Understanding the material. Stone is a product of nature. As such, it will have varying color and veining patterns, even within a single tile. These should not be viewed as imperfections but rather as the natural expression of the material. If a more uniform look is desired, homeowners should look for stones that feature less variation and a more consistent look from tile to tile or within a single piece. Moreover, homeowners should request samples of the desired stone material. Since a 4 x 4-inch sample of a stone will not generally demonstrate the variety that can occur in a larger slab or tile, homeowners should request 12 x 12-inch samples and enough samples to show the range that can be found within a single stone.

Given the unique characteristics of natural stone, it is important to rely on experienced stone distributors and installers who understand the nuances of the material.

Comparative costs of stone. A common misconception about natural stone is that it is economically prohibitive when compared to other materials. While the initial cost of natural stone is higher than lower-end products such as linoleum, it is comparable with man-made products such as ceramic tiles or solid surfaces.

Moreover, the life cycle of natural stone is much greater than virtually all man-made materials—from an aesthetic standpoint as well as a practical view. Stone floors and countertops have a timelessness that rarely goes out of style, making replacement unlikely. And the high durability and low maintenance of natural stone ensures that the initial cost of natural stone is well recouped over time.

Specialized labor. For masonry applications, the need for an experienced stonemason is critical. Proper installation of stone masonry is truly an art form, and a skilled mason can greatly enhance a residential project. However, an unskilled mason can make even the best stone products look poor in the final application. As with any specialized contracting work, homeowners should ask for references and should view examples or photos of a stonemason's completed work.

In the area of stone tiles, although the adhesives and grout used for installation are the same as those used for ceramic tile,

While many kitchen countertops tend to be polished granite, marble with a honed finish offers another option. This kitchen features honed Verde marble, which evokes a feeling of subdued elegance.

Stone Supplier:
   **Walker Zanger,
   Sylmar, California**

there are exceptions for certain stone materials, and a homeowner must rely on the experience of the contractor to recognize these exceptions. For example, many green marbles—which are actually serpentine in geological classification—are subject to warping when installed with traditional adhesives. Therefore, an epoxy adhesive is often required to install green marble tiles for a residential floor. Also, the homeowner must rely on the experience of the stone installer to ensure that the substrate can support the additional weight of a natural stone floor.

However, even though experience with natural stone is necessary, the overall installation cost for stone tiles should not be higher than the cost for installing ceramic tile. In general, the man-hours required to install a stone floor are no more than the time needed to install a ceramic tile floor.

This is also generally true for stone countertops, which require a great deal of expertise from the stone contractor. It is strongly advised to make sure that the same firm is responsible for measuring, fabricating and installing all of the kitchen countertops and/or bathroom vanity tops. Relying on multiple contractors for a single countertop project increases the chances of miscalculations or misinterpretation of the measurements among the different firms. Also, an experienced stone contractor will make sure the cabinetry that will be supporting the countertops can sustain the weight of the material.

How much stone is appropriate? Building a "stone house" does not necessarily mean that stone will be used throughout a residence. The amount of stone can vary greatly, depending on budget and the overall aesthetic desire of the homeowner. Exterior stonework can include entire elevations of natural stone, or it can be limited to a stone base, or stonework for feature elements, such as door and window surrounds. In general, stone works best when it is used in areas where it can be "experienced" by those around it. Upon approaching a stone wall—particularly textured stone—there is an overwhelming desire to reach out and touch the material, which is why it is advisable to use it in areas where it can not only be seen but also felt.

Inside a residence, homeowners are specifying natural stone for more traditional applications, such as kitchens, bathrooms, and fireplaces, and they are also using it in living areas and entryways. With more residences being built with an "open" floor plan, natural stone can become a unifying element throughout a home, tying together different spaces.

Man-made options. Following the increased popularity of natural stone, manufacturers of man-made materials such as ceramic tiles and solid surfaces (i.e., DuPont Corian, DuPont Zodiaq and similar products) are creating coverings that mimic the appearance of natural stone. These materials offer many of the same practical advantages as natural stone, such as high durability and easy maintenance. Additionally, as mass-produced products, they offer an extremely high level of consistency in size and thickness.

However, these items may not be effective for homeowners seeking a one-of-a-kind look. Although the process of creating these stone-look products has advanced in recent times, they remain a manufactured material without the unique characteristics of natural stone. (See the chapter "Stone-Look Materials" for a more detailed look at manufactured stone-look products.)

Stone Outside

When building a residence, it often seems that emphasis is placed on the interior design. But selecting the materials for the exterior of the home should also be a high priority. In addition to the façade, other areas to consider include the driveway, staircases, walkways, patio, retaining walls and landscape. And, just as with interior design, the type of stone and finish that is chosen plays a significant role in setting the tone of the home.

Even if budget constraints don't allow for an entire stone-faced exterior, there are other outdoor areas where stone features can be used to dress up a property. Using stone pavers for a driveway or walkway is just one way to enhance the look of a home's exterior. Pavers are also a great option for a patio or pool deck. Another consideration is to use large pieces of slate to create a pathway—giving the home a more rustic feel.

Fieldstone is another popular choice for outdoor design. While all varieties of natural stone are extracted from the earth, fieldstone has an inherent quality that truly relates to the land. Perhaps it is because each region across the country and around the world has its own distinctive stone with its unique texture and blend of colors. And it is most likely because of these traits that fieldstone is a prevalent choice in outdoor designs.

Many of the reasons for choosing fieldstone are the same from project to project. One common thread among projects is the desire to reflect a natural setting. "Our typical work reflects the vernacular of the area," said architect Robert

Approximately 130 tons of northern California fieldstone, which is volcanic in nature, was specified for this California home. "It was attached to the concrete foundation with dowels," said Kevin Kearney, builder and owner. The pathways and decks are made of China Green slate from Echeguren Slate. The green color of the slate blends well with the natural surroundings.

Designer/General Contractor: **Kearney & O'Banion Design, San Francisco, California**
Masonry Contractor/Stone Installer: **Robert Feenan Masonry, Windsor, California**
Roofing Contractor: **St. John Roofing, Napa, California**
Stone Supplier: **Echeguren Slate, San Francisco, California**
Photo: **David Duncan Livingston**

Orr of Robert Orr & Associates in New Haven, Connecticut. "We take great pains to immerse ourselves in the locale, to find how people have done things for years. We use fieldstone quite often for projects scattered around the country." The architect explains that in each case, he and his design team go in search of a local supplier and an experienced stonemason.

The objective for one new residence designed by Orr in the mountains of central New Jersey was to give the impression that the home had undergone

several renovations through the years. The use of local fieldstone played a key role in achieving this effect.

"We were trying to make it look like an old farmhouse that had grown over time," said Orr. "We made it look like there was a small house that was added onto as the family grew and prospered. The stonemason's technique of stonework fit beautifully with this concept. He used colored grout to make it look like it had been there forever."

The design plans originally specified 4-inch-thick pieces of stone for the

exterior façade, with larger stones on the corners to give the illusion of more thickness. "We had actually designed the house for stone veneer," Orr said. "We assumed the stonemason would be buying the stone on a pallet. When he looked at the drawings, he came back saying he would have to charge more money because he would have to cut down all the stone. His pieces were 8 or 9 inches thick. We said, 'That's great,' and agreed to change the drawings to accommodate the thicker stone."

The fieldstone clads the entire exterior of the 6,500-square-foot main house. The property also includes a barn/guest house and a pool house, which

For a new residence in the mountains of central New Jersey, the objective was to give the impression that the home had undergone several renovations through the years. The use of local fieldstone is a key component in achieving this effect. "We were trying to make it look like an old farmhouse that had expanded over time," said Orr, "that there was a small house added as the family grew and prospered. The stonemason's technique of stonework fit in beautifully with this concept. He used colored grout to make it look like it had been there forever."

"We had actually designed the house for stone veneer," said the architect. "We assumed the stonemason would be buying the stone on a pallet. When he looked at the drawings, he came back saying he would have to charge more money because he would have to recut all the stone to smaller sizes. His pieces were 8 or 9 inches thick. We said, 'That's great,' and agreed to change the drawings to accommodate the thicker stone."

Architect: **Robert Orr & Associates, New Haven, Connecticut**
Stonemason: **Marty Faulborn**
Photos: **Photo Communications, Inc.**

total about another 2,500 square feet. "It was a lot of stonework," said Orr, adding that fieldstone was also employed for walls, patios and paving.

Orr explained that the local mason salvages a lot of his stone from old barns. "He picked through his piles and always got just the right stone for the right place," said the architect, adding that the mason was very thorough in his work. "The pavers looked like big flat stones with grass around them, but each stone was 2 feet thick. He put them in with equipment. His way of doing things had such good aesthetics. Working with the stonemason was actually a real learning experience. We often work with veneer. It was refreshing to have a job that had the integrity of using thicker stone."

Stone accents

If a complete stone-faced exterior façade—such as the one Orr designed for the New Jersey residence—is not a budgetary option, there is always the possibility of accenting the exterior with a stone foundation or roof. This was the case for one homeowner in Sebastopol, California, who reconstructed his home to reflect the nineteenth-century American shingle-style homes of the East Coast, which included a fair amount of stonework—especially slate.

Exemplified by McKim, Mead and White—the renowned New England architectural firm of the late nineteenth century—this shingle style was nostalgic for Kevin Kearney, president of Kearney & O'Banion, Inc., who served as chief designer and general contractor for his home project. "Where I grew up in Maryland, a lot of the houses had old stone foundations," Kearney said. "It was a working-class Irish neighborhood in Baltimore, where our house was brick and had a slate roof. They are considered expensive building materials today, but everyone used these materials to build their houses back then because they would last forever. It's a look I came to appreciate and still love."

Kearney was also influenced by Bernard Maybeck, an architect who brought this New England shingle-style home to California in the late nineteenth century. According to the designer, Maybeck even used an abundance of slate in his projects to fit the region's nature-inspired environment.

"Another thing that led me to this decision was that in a large house, a lot of what you see is the roof," Kearney said. "Most modern materials don't add

The stonemason who supplied the fieldstone for the New Jersey project salvages much of his building material from old barns. "He picked through his piles and always got just the right stone for the right place," said Orr.

Photo:
Photo Communications, Inc.

26

anything aesthetically to the building. In fact, you're lucky if they don't take something away. Slate adds an aesthetic dimension that, in my opinion, nothing else does."

The surroundings of the California residence also played a factor in the redesign. "We have one hundred to two hundred mature redwood trees on our nine-acre property," Kearney said. "Stone and wood shingles lend themselves to this natural atmosphere. We wanted a modern home and all of the features of a smart house, but we wanted a home that within a few years would look like it had been there for quite a while. Our goal was to create a generational home."

The park-like setting of the home also affected Kearney's decision of what type of slate to use. "The stone we used is China Green slate," he said. "We used about one hundred squares of roofing slate and at

Heavily influenced by the nineteenth-century American shingle-style home of the East Coast, this California residence includes a great amount of stonework. The slate roof and pathways, combined with a fieldstone foundation, complement the wood shingles well.

Designer/General Contractor: **Kearney & O'Banion Design, San Francisco, California**
Masonry Contractor/Stone Installer: **Robert Feenan Masonry, Windsor, California**
Roofing Contractor: **St. John Roofing, Napa, California**
Stone Supplier: **Echeguren Slate, San Francisco, California**
Photo: **David Duncan Livingston**

least sixty tons of it for the decks. The green color fits in well with the surroundings." The decks were laid in 24 x 24-inch squares, while the walking paths and ground-floor decks used the same slate in a random pattern.

From a structural standpoint, the residence stands three stories tall and is built into a hill. At the front of the home, one full story is underground. The foundation was built accordingly, so from the rear, 10 feet of stone is visible, while in the front, only $2^{1}/2$ feet of the stone can be seen. Fieldstone was selected for the foundation, a choice influenced by the homes of the East Coast and especially the New England area. "It was attached to the concrete foundation with dowels," Kearney said. "Above the foundation is a redwood water table about 12 inches wide, and the shingles start above that." Approximately 130 tons of northern California fieldstone, which is volcanic in nature, was specified for this project.

The decks surrounding the Sebastopol home required approximately 60 tons of slate. The flooring in these areas was laid in 24 x 24-inch squares, while the walking paths and ground-floor decks used the same slate in a random pattern.

The residence stands three stories tall and is built into a hill. At the front of the home, one full story is underground. The foundation was built accordingly; from the rear, 10 feet of stone is visible, while in the front, only $2^{1}/2$ feet of stone can be seen.

Photos: **David Duncan Livingston**

A random-patterned slate patio around the pool adds a touch of elegance to this residence. The varying sized, multicolored tiles not only are aesthetically pleasing, but the rough texture of the material ensures a slip-resistant surface.

Stone Supplier: **Diniz Design, Baton Rouge, Louisiana**

Random pieces of rough-cut Durango Stone were used as paving around this pool area, and the same material was also used for the Jacuzzi steps and surround. The light tones of the Durango Stone contrast with rough boulders at the waterfall and dark brick facing of the Jacuzzi.

Stone Supplier: **World Wide Stone Corp., Phoenix, Arizona**

Tying to the environment

Sharing a similar design goal as Kearney, the owners of a home in New Canaan, Connecticut, also desired to use building materials that reflected the natural environment. Designed by Louise Brooks, ASLA, of the New Canaan firm of Gullans & Brooks Associates, Inc., the renovation included greatly expanding an existing house, while siting it in a much more environmentally friendly way.

"We wanted to create different areas around the house," Brooks said, "and yet have it sit on a nice plateau." The idea was to gain a finished look using cut stone, but to keep the house part of its environment.

"We definitely wanted the structure to fit into its surroundings," Brooks continued. "But we didn't try to match the stone on the existing house, which is more granite-like."

Brooks and landscape architect Keith Simpson of Keith Simpson Associates also created a pool and terraced staircase at one end of the building, which "grounds" the house.

For this Connecticut residence, local fieldstone and New York bluestone were used at the lower levels to incorporate the structure into the surrounding environment.

For this residence in New Canaan, Connecticut, local fieldstone and New York bluestone were used at the lower levels to incorporate the structure into the surrounding environment. The design goal was to achieve a finished look using cut stone and to ensure that the house remained part of its natural setting.

The outdoor design of the home illustrates how natural stone has taken a prominent position in landscape design, as it has been used to relate the residence to its natural surroundings. A pool and terraced staircase at one end of the home were built to "ground" the structure.

Architect: **Gullans & Brooks Associates, Inc., New Canaan, Connecticut**
Contractor: **Stasio, Inc., Ridgefield, Connecticut**
Supplier: **Bedford Stone, Bedford, New York**

Reflecting a region

Rich in history and a strong tradition of building with limestone, the Mankato region of Minnesota is an area treasured by many of its residents. In particular, it evokes special memories for architect Rick Lundin and his family. As a way of preserving these memories, Lundin designed a home for his parents in Madison Lake, Minnesota, that incorporates native stone as well as images of his family and the region's industrial past.

Although stone plays an important role in the design because of its beauty and regional relationship, the reason the owners chose Northern Buff Minnesota limestone from Vetter Stone Co. burrows even deeper. According to Lundin of CONstruct Architects in Minneapolis, Minnesota, "Vetter and my family's business have often had a near-symbiotic relationship. My family has been in the highway construction business since 1910 and has always quarried its own limestone for road-base material. Our quarries are adjacent to Vetter's location, and we tend to work with each other's quarries on occasion. The beauty of Vetter stone goes beyond aesthetics. It is the material my family has built our foundations on for nearly a hundred years."

When designing his parents' 5,000-square-foot home, Lundin planned for the primary mass of the residence to resemble an aged barn foundation. "In this region, there was a strong tradition of building barn foundations with the local limestone," he said. "Our desire is that a visitor to the site would be struck with the thought that a building had existed here one hundred years ago."

Northern Buff Minnesota limestone with various finishes was used throughout this 5,000-square-foot residence in Madison Lake, Minnesota. The exterior of the home was designed to resemble an aged-barn foundation, which was a local tradition of architecture in the region.

Owners:	**Richard and Darlene Lundin, Madison Lake, Minnesota**
Architect:	**CONstruct Architects, Minneapolis, Minnesota**
Landscape Architect:	**Herb Baldwin, Jordan, Minnesota**
Interior Design:	**Christine Walthour, Minneapolis, Minnesota**
General Contractor:	**General Contractor Inc., Mankato, Minnesota**
Stone Installer:	**Paul Groebner, Mankato, Minnesota**
Stone Installer/Supplier:	**Big Fun Works, Minneapolis, Minnesota (countertops and floor)**
Stone Supplier:	**Vetter Stone Co., Kasota, Minnesota (limestone)**
Landscape/Retaining Wall Installer:	**Southern Minnesota Construction, Mankato, Minnesota**

As Lundin explained it, the home sits on top of a hill, bounded on one side by rolling prairies and fields and by water on the other. "The public views the house from the rolling field side," he said. "That's where you encounter most of the stone. We wanted to convey a feeling of permanence and a sense of anchoring. The house is more dynamic on the lake side, with a curving roof supported by light steel trusses."

To embellish the century-old look of the property, Lundin placed reject quarry stones along an existing ridgeline on the site. "The old quarry stones were placed in a way that recalls an old stone outcropping one would find in the quarries and prairies surrounding the Mankato region," he said. "Other unique stones were scattered throughout the site. One such stone is a piece of limestone with a naturally carved bowl that is used to catch rainwater from the gutters. In the old glacial rivers, a piece of hard granite would get caught and swirled around against the softer limestone, carving out a natural bowl. Amazingly, a nearly perfect round piece of granite still rests in the base of the bowl."

From design through installation, the project took about two years to complete. "It was a very rewarding project," said Lundin, "a wonderful opportunity to work so closely with my parents and to be able to build a home that, while deeply rooted in family and local history, finds new expression for those ideas. My most satisfying moments are watching my parents taking visitors on a tour through the house, and seeing how new understandings of the family and architecture are revealed through the wood and stone."

For this residence along the banks of the Delaware River in New Hope, Pennsylvania, the exterior is comprised of Delaware Valley Sandstone.

In addition to sandstone cladding, natural stone was also used for the paving around the pool area.

Laid-up stone

After deciding to use natural stone for an exterior façade of a residence, the next decision is to determine how thick the stone pieces should be. The size of the pieces used can make all the difference in how long the job will take and what type of installation method will be implemented.

While most people would probably favor an exterior built of thick stone blocks, there is time and money to consider. "There is a big difference between a veneer and a laid-up stone," said J. Robert Hillier, FAIA, of The Hillier Group in Princeton, New Jersey. "I think the diamond saw saved the stone industry to a large extent, because it was able to take stone and turn it into sheets. But those sheets are handled entirely differently than laid-up stone, and I think that's a big factor. Laymen don't know that. They look at a one-inch-thick stone wall, and they think it was done like the old days."

But even if the budget only allows for veneer, there are ways to give the impression that the stone façade is thicker than it really is. This look can be achieved by installing thicker blocks at the corners. "Put your money where it's important," said Hillier. "For old barns, there were always 'corner men,' who were the stonecutters that laid up the corners. If you ever look at an old barn, you'll see that the stone on the corners is always carefully cut, and it's all rubble in between. This is because you build the corners, and then the laborers would throw the stone in between. That's something that escapes a lot of architects."

This philosophy was in place for a residence Hillier designed along the banks of the Delaware River in New Hope, Pennsylvania. The residence—dubbed Autretemps—utilizes Delaware Valley sandstone for the

The rough-textured sandstone was specified for all exterior elevations of the structure, while following the classic tradition of exterior rough stone installation. The corners are the most detailed elements.

exterior. Using skilled stonemasons, the sandstone was laid stone upon stone, with larger pieces at the corners. To complement the sandstone cladding, which was used for several exterior elevations, the design also includes natural stone as paving around the pool area. The combination of natural stone varieties on the exterior gave the project a rough-hewn feel that complemented the historic nature of the surroundings, as well as a feeling of refinement.

Architect: **The Hillier Group, Princeton, New Jersey**
Stone Supplier: **Delaware Quarries, Lumberville, Pennsylvania**

Inspired by nature

In his design for Trapps Gateway, which is situated at the entry point to New York State's largest privately funded preserve, architect Lee H. Skolnick wanted a structure that would not encroach upon the surrounding environment. Built using Shawangunk conglomerate stone extracted from the site and nearby cliffs, the building gently blended into the landscape.

"We very much understood that the mission of the preserve was contradictory to building on the land, so we wanted to make a place that had as little impact on the land as possible," Skolnick said. "For that reason, we buried half of the building into the slope, so when you approach it, all you see are these big stone blocks and an overhead roof."

To minimize the aesthetic impact, the site for the building was carefully considered. "We sited the center along the glacial erratics, which were formed tens of thousands of years ago," the architect explained. "The stone of the building is aligned to give the impression that it came out of the earth."

And while the architecture of the building helped it merge with the surroundings, the choice of stone was also a key factor. "The stone was a conglomerate from the site itself or from the immediate vicinity," Skolnick said. "It's an incredibly strong material that's been described as 'nature's concrete.' It was made from glacial movement pressing stones together until they formed a solid block."

According to Skolnick, the appearance of the stone will adjust with time. "It weathers in a very pleasing way," he said. "Some of it is startlingly white when it comes out of the ground, but it does acquire a patina due to the minerals. This makes for a variegated surface, with some red and some white, and there are moss and lichens that grow on it."

To bring the project to reality, Skolnick relied on the skill of his contractor, Storm King Contracting in Montgomery, New York. "We were blessed with a local mason who comes from a long line of stonemasons," he said.

In designing Trapps Gateway, which is located in rural New York State, architect Lee H. Skolnick wanted a facility that would not encroach upon the surrounding environment. Shawangunk conglomerate stone, extracted from the site and nearby cliffs, allows the building to gently blend into the landscape.

To have as little impact on the land as possible, half of the building is buried in the slope of the landscape.

To achieve the desired look, the architect and stonemasons worked closely together, forming mock-ups before actual construction began.

In addition to the building itself, the stones were used around the site for retaining walls and screen beds to divert water from higher elevations.

Architect: **Lee H. Skolnick Architecture + Design Partnership, New York, New York**
General Contractor/Construction Manager: **Storm King Contracting, Montgomery, New York**
Mechanical Engineer: **Altieri Sebor Wiebor, Norwalk, Connecticut**
Structural and Civil Engineering: **Medenback & Eggers, Stone Ridge, New York**
Landscape Architect: **Hudson and Pacific Designs, Inc., Kingston, New York**

"He found stones around the site. For the entry area, he found a stone that came in the shape of a bench. It didn't even have to be carved. They brought up old mill stones during the excavation and placed them at strategic points." The construction of the project took approximately one year, including a great deal of site work.

To achieve the desired look, the architect and stonemasons worked closely together. "There were a lot of mock-ups and samples. Because of the nature of the project, there was no model we could point to and say, 'Do the stone in this manner.' We wanted a broad variety, with large and small stones near each other. The mason would do mock-ups of large sections of wall, and I would point to sections I liked and didn't like; we did this with the whole crew."

In addition to the building itself, the stone was used for retaining walls and screen beds to divert water from higher elevations. "Again, mock-ups were done to make sure it didn't look like dressed stone," the architect said. "The corners weren't uniform."

The cost of extracting the stone from the site was offset by the fact that the material did not have to be paid for. "There was an expense working with such odd-shaped stones. Some were heavy, and it was very labor-intensive," Skolnick said. "But the material cost us nothing, and it couldn't have been better aesthetically. The purpose of the project left us no choice. We couldn't bring Pennsylvania fieldstone to Mohonk."

To enhance the natural look, the masons tried to avoid letting the mortar show. "The mortar they used was hidden, and there were some dry-laid walls," Skolnick said. "We talked through the details and left the final decisions to the mason. A lot of the site work was determined in the field."

For the roof, the architect chose gray-green slate. "We wanted something that lent itself to that particular landscape, and this slate works with the colors of the cliffs and vegetation of the area," Skolnick said. "We wanted something that would be maintenance-free and would look timeless right from the beginning. The concept of the building was to use all natural material, and putting anything else up just didn't make sense."

Emulating the environment

By carefully considering the natural surroundings and the history of the area, architect Paul Edwards was able to make it appear that the Estates at Honey Bee Ridge in Oro Valley, Arizona, had stood for decades. The design, which was derived from a pattern of Anasazi Indian pottery found in northern Arizona, is similar to that of the nearby Hohokam ruins, and utilizes Kiva forms, fire pits and weathered stone to match the natural outcroppings in the area.

The site, which offers spectacular views of the Santa Catalina and Tortolita Mountains, is "surrounded by unearthly rock formations and stately saguaro cacti," explained Edwards, who added that boulders from the area were incorporated into the design to "create a lasting sense of place." The boulders were

By carefully considering the natural surroundings and the history of the area, architect Paul Edwards was able to make it appear that the Estates at Honey Bee Ridge in Oro Valley, Arizona, had stood for decades. The design, which was derived from a pattern of Anasazi Indian pottery found in northern Arizona, is similar to that of the nearby Hohokam ruins.

The design of Honey Bee Ridge in Arizona utilizes weathered stone quarried locally to emulate the natural outcroppings in the area.

The stone was used in a broad range of sizes, with its weathered surface enhancing the overall design goal.

The sandstone continues around the soffits and window ledges. This was a challenge as the mason didn't want these items to look "too perfect," and the stone had to fit in the window ledges as naturally as possible.

found during the construction of the road leading into the development, and the stone veneer was laid on top to make it appear as a boulder outcropping.

For the exterior façades, a sandstone from Ashfork, Arizona, called Rito Vistoso stone, was utilized throughout the structure. "The weathered side of the stone (as opposed to the sawn surface of the stone) was used on the outside of the gatehouse to help maintain the sense of history in the area and to create respect for it," according to Edwards.

In addition to the immediate aesthetic benefits of using Arizona sandstone, the architect also pointed to the long-term advantages. "We wanted materials that would age well," he said, adding that some of the stones had lichen on them, enhancing the sense of timelessness.

In siting the project, one goal was to blend the structure into the ruins of the area. To achieve this, the building was given a triangular shape with a slope towards the top to make it look like a ruin. This proved effective because of the communication between the owner, the architect, the civil engineers and the mason. They would all meet together and "bounce ideas off each other."

One design detail—a notch in the roof—offered practical as well as aesthetic benefits, as it created a colorful mark on the stone and would also help prevent water from accumulating. The fire pits also served a dual purpose: functioning as elements of the home and recalling the rituals of Native Americans of the region.

The use of stone continues for the soffits and window ledges. This was a challenge during the project, as the mason didn't want these items to look "too perfect," and the stone had to fit in the window ledges as naturally as possible.

Architect: **CDG Architects, Tucson, Arizona**
Landscape Architect: **WLB Landscape Architects, Tucson, Arizona**
Contractor: **Louis Marson & Sons, Inc., Scottsdale, Arizona**
Stone Supplier: **Dunbar Stone, Ashfork, Arizona**
Masonry Contractor: **D & B Masonry, Tucson, Arizona**

The owners of this European-style residence in California lavished as much attention on the exterior details of the property as they did on the interior spaces. Clockwise, from left: paths of Utah Blonde wind their way around the gardens; even the lowly mailbox gets the grand treatment with its roof of China Multi Slate copper edging and veneering of Rustic Santa Barbara Sandstone; the barbeque is situated just outside the casement windows of the kitchen; a private Jacuzzi off the master bedroom features a pre-cast concrete lion-head fountain by Gianninni; the spectacular "family" Jacuzzi is surrounded with Natural Brown Round boulders; a stone garden bench is quietly absorbed by the surrounding plantings.

Owners: **Jack and Vicki Kerns**
Landscape Architect: **Jack Kerns**
Contractor: **D. W. Johnson Construction, Inc., Palm Springs, California**
Landscape Installation: **Hort Tech, Palm Springs, California**
Stone Supplier: **Modern Building Materials, Cathedral City, California**
Photos: **Kurt Wahlner**

Stone Inside

The use of stone in residential interiors can take on many forms. Some homes may be designed with natural stone for a featured area, such as an entryway or fireplace, with more modest materials throughout the remainder of the residence. Other homeowners may choose to implement stone in all areas of the home, even using the material as a unifying element from room to room and within hallways.

Once homeowners make the choice of stone for their residence, they find that the material serves as much more than an upscale alternative to ceramic tile, carpeting or hardwood. Designers are using natural stone to express the tastes and, more importantly, the personalities of the people who reside in a home. Indeed, the use of stone has become a very personal statement by the home owners, revealing how they view themselves.

With the variety of natural stone products that have hit the marketplace over the past decade, homeowners are choosing from an expanded color palette that includes more shades and tones than ever before. Moreover, the many stone varieties available today allow consumers to have a broad range of color even within a single material.

Conversely, the desire for a muted palette of neutral stone has remained popular for some time now. It allows the stone to serve as the framework for a setting, thus giving the homeowner an opportunity to introduce new furnishings or fabrics in a space without fear of clashing with the existing stonework.

The variety of mosaic possibilities can be seen in this Florida residence. The home features a very open floor plan, with crosscut travertine floor tiles used throughout. At the entry, a circular medallion was installed with stone mosaic pieces that include shades of dark green, light green, beige, tan and off-white.

Designer: **Romanza Architectural Interiors, Orlando, Florida**
Photo: **Laurence Taylor**

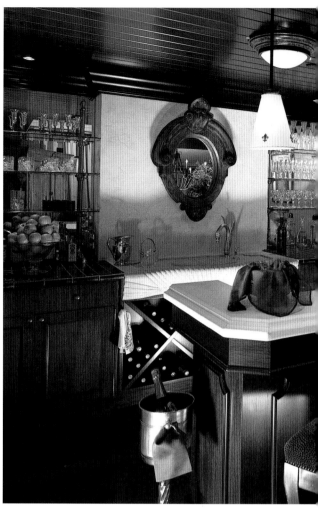

In this residential hallway, the design includes lime-stone, marble and Noce travertine—all with a tumbled finish—to serve as a background material for the rich mahogany woodwork that was used for the cabinetry, doors, furnishings and ceilings. The same stone materials were also used for a small mosaic medallion, which serves as a focal element without overwhelming the space.

Homeowners are boldly using materials such as lime-stone for new applications. For this bar area, Alhambra limestone was used for the countertop as well as for the sink, and both elements have withstood extensive use since being installed. "The owners have maybe three parties a season with ninety people in the house, and the bar there is used like any bar in any New York restaurant," said the designer. "It really gets used, and the owners have not had a problem."

Interior Designer: **Calder Interiors, New York, New York**
Stone Supplier: **Elizabeth Street Gardens, New York, New York**
Photo: **Philip H. Ennis**

Choosing buff tones

Homeowners who want to use natural stone without it becoming the focal element of a residence are often led to use off-white materials, including limestone, travertine and certain varieties of marble. While limestone is generally considered to be a porous material, that does not limit its design value, explains designer Nicholas Calder of New York–based Calder Interiors. "It depends on the area that it's going into, the wear factors, and the end result that you are looking for," he said.

Calder points to one residential project where he specified a bar top of Alhambra limestone. "The owners have maybe three parties a season with ninety people in the

house, and the bar there is used like any bar in any New York restaurant," he said. "It really gets used, and the owners have not had a problem. Even if it were to get a ring, the client could always get it refinished, but that hasn't happened."

The same residential bar area also features a sink made of carved limestone, which has held up as well as the bar top, according to Calder. "Everything—including whiskey, scotch, water and wine—all goes down the drain, and it holds up well," he said.

Like many design options, applications for limestone and other light-colored stones depend on the client. When using stone as a background element for a residence, the effect of neutral-colored stones can be enhanced by the finish given to the material. When seeking this aesthetic for residential projects, Calder has often selected a "tumbled" or honed finish for marble flooring, which is more muted than a polished surface. One example includes the use of limestone, marble and Noce traver-

In this residential living area, a floor-to-ceiling fireplace is comprised of Roman travertine. The unfilled travertine, which was quarried in Italy, features contemporary detailing for the surround and mantel. Even while the fireplace is the centerpiece of the room, it blends gently with the other design elements—such as the curtain fabrics, furnishings and wall paint—all of which feature soft coloring to complement the stone.

Interior Designer:
  **Calder Interiors,
  New York, New York**
Photo: **Philip H. Ennis**

tine—all with a tumbled finish—to serve as background material for the rich mahogany woodwork that was used for the cabinetry, doors, furnishings and even the ceilings. In the corridor of this residence, Calder chose to combine the three materials in a small mosaic medallion that serves as a focal element without overwhelming the space.

For another residence, Calder selected Roman travertine to comprise a floor-to-ceiling fireplace unit. The unfilled travertine, which was quarried in Italy, features contemporary detailing on the surround and mantel. But even while the fireplace is the centerpiece of the room, it blends gently with other design elements such as the curtains, furnishings and wall paint, all of which feature soft coloring to complement the stone.

Contrasting light and dark

Even when a homeowner selects a neutral-colored stone as the predominant flooring element, this does not completely preclude the use of darker stone materials. Homeowners are contrasting the light field tiles with darker accents in a variety of formats. These have ranged from simple accent dot tiles set on the diagonal to borders and even two-toned "stone carpets," where light and dark stones are combined in a featured area such as an entranceway.

It is also possible to select light-colored stones that feature a contrast within the surface. Many stone types have subtle veining patterns that run across the surface, breaking up the stark plane of the stone.

Both of these contrasting factors come into play in a condominium on the Florida coast. In this space, the homeowners selected Crema Europa limestone as the primary flooring element. The stone, which was quarried in Spain, was used predominantly as large-format tiles measuring 24 x 24 inches each. In addition, the stone was used for stair treads and risers throughout the residence.

But even while the design includes large, uninterrupted areas of flooring that solely feature the Crema Europa tiles, the stone provides subtle variation due to the natural veining on the surface, which is slightly darker and gives the material an almost windblown appearance.

At the entryway, an even more dramatic contrast is provided by the introduction of Absolute Black granite. In this area, the granite frames a rectangular area along the curved glass wall, forming a large "welcome mat" in natural stone. To add visual interest, three 4 x 4-inch accent tiles of Absolute Black granite are set on the diagonal within the rectangular border.

Mosaics were used for the fireplace in the living room. This mosaic border pattern picks up a portion of the entry mosaic, using the dark green, light green and off-white pieces.

Designer:
**Romanza Architectural
Interiors, Orlando, Florida**
Photo:
Laurence Taylor

A free-flowing look

Some homeowners have discovered the flexibility of stone mosaics, which "are ideal for curved surfaces such as arched openings because you can get that free-flowing look," says designer Chad Moor of Romanza Architectural Interiors in Orlando, Florida. "They are a design element that allows for flexibility, and they follow the curves perfectly."

Materials used to create mosaic art vary and include colored glass, ceramic tile and even mirror fragments, but natural stone is still a prevalent choice for many designers. "Most of the mosaics we do are stone," Moor says. "It gives a natural old-world look and blends with other natural stones found in the majority of our flooring."

The variety of mosaic possibilities can be seen in one Florida residence designed by Romanza. The home features a very open floor plan, with crosscut travertine floor tiles used throughout. In addition, mosaics were designed in two areas of interest. At the entry, a circular medallion was installed with stone mosaic pieces that include shades of dark green, light green, beige, tan and off-white.

Mosaics were also used for the fireplace in the living room. This mosaic border pattern picks up a portion of the entry mosaic, using the dark green, light green and off-white pieces.

Providing an open feel

The natural tones of stone can also contribute a light, airy feel to a space, particularly when using white marble. For a private residence in Birmingham, Alabama, large quantities of Colorado Yule Gold Vein marble were utilized with accents of Alabama Pink marble. Because of the high ceilings and wide expanses of marble on the floor, visitors to the home feel as though they have not left the outdoors.

Before this project became a reality, the homeowner split with her original designer and relied on the savvy of contractor Greg Gibbs. "We talked through the project, and after the original designer wouldn't sketch anything for her, she asked if I could build the house from my sketches," he says, adding that there was a great deal of communication throughout the process. "The homeowner described what she wanted, and I would go home and sketch it. Then I would put it up in 3-D on computer, bring it over to her, and she would approve it that way or make changes." The entire project, from design to completion of construction, took a total of fourteen months.

Once the homeowner chose Colorado Yule marble as the main flooring

This private residence in Birmingham, Alabama, features wide expanses of Colorado Yule Gold Vein marble on the floor. Combined with high ceilings and abundant natural light, the stone gives the space an open airy feel.

In addition to the Colorado Yule marble, the home features accents of Alabama Pink marble as a balancing material and also as a tribute to the owner's home state. In addition to serving as a flooring accent, Alabama Pink was used in large-format pieces for the fireplace surround.

Builder:
  Greg Gibbs Construction Co., Maylene, Alabama
Stone Supplier:
  IGM, Atlanta, Georgia
Photos:
  Steve Hogben Photography

material, Alabama Pink was selected as a balancing material and also as a tribute to her home state. In addition to serving as a flooring accent, Alabama Pink was used in large-format pieces for the fireplace surround. The Colorado Yule marble was utilized primarily as 12 x 12-inch tiles and was installed over a period of six weeks.

Replicating a castle

In conceiving a design for the sunroom of her home, Karen Grierson sought to create a perfect replica of an old European castle. The theme of the room—a 500-year trip back in time—is carried out through a combination of marble varieties, with inserts, intensive faux painting and special lighting. The entire ceiling of the room is covered with 3 x 3-foot panels of marble mosaic, created by a mosaic artist who studied Renaissance art. Each panel contains marble, granite and semi-precious stones set on a grid and custom-framed with an elegant crown molding that has been faux-painted to add to the antique effect. The walls of the room are covered in 6 x 6-inch tumbled travertine that was color-enhanced after installation to bring out the rich gold tone of the stone.

Because the tiles were not grouted, every corner intersection had to be filled with a special mixture of three colors of grout to blend with the natural stone color and avert dark voids or spot effects.

A red marble fireplace wall, enhanced by a limestone mantel with mosaic inserts, further enhances the room's ancient "castle-like" effect. Architectural columns are covered in ³/₄-inch-thick polished golden travertine, grouted with a mallard green color. Three entrance arches, creating a transition between the new room and the rest of the house, have sides made from hand-carved golden marble from Bulgaria.

For the floor, the homeowner selected a combination of 16 x 16-inch tumbled travertine and 3 x 3-inch handmade Seneca tiles. The floor was left ungrouted to perpetuate the theme, and every corner was cut to introduce a 4 x 4-inch tumbled Giallo marble insert. The entire floor was mud-set over cork underlay, then enhanced and sealed multiple times to bring out the rich gold tone of the stone.

Designer: **Thorning Little**
Stone Supplier: **South West Tile, Sarasota, Florida**
Stone Contractor: **Atlantic Tile & Marble Inc., Sarasota, Florida**
General Contractor: **Bill Christie**
Photo: **Coverings**

In conceiving a design for the sunroom of her home, Karen Grierson sought to create a replica of an old European castle. The theme of the room—a 500-year trip back in time—is carried out through a combination of marbles taken to the extreme, with inserts, intensive faux painting and special lighting. The entire ceiling of the room is covered with 3 x 3-foot panels of marble mosaic, created by a mosaic artist who studied Renaissance art. Each panel contains marble, granite and semiprecious stones, set on a grid and custom-

framed with an elegant crown molding that has been faux-painted to add to the antique effect.

For the floor, Karen selected a combination of 16 x 16-inch tumbled travertine and 3 x 3-inch handmade Seneca tiles. The floor was left ungrouted to perpetuate the theme, and every corner was cut to introduce a 4 x 4-inch tumbled Giallo marble insert. The entire floor was mud set over cork underlay, then enhanced and sealed multiple times to bring out the rich gold tone of the stone.

53

A connecting point

When planning the design for an upscale residence in Deal, New Jersey, the design goal was to create a look recalling Tuscan themes from centuries past. This was done by combining stone with rich-looking maple and mahogany woods throughout. In addition to providing a classical look, the stone tied the living spaces with the kitchen and dining areas.

"We wanted to make it look like an old eighteenth- or nineteenth-century house on the Mediterranean," said designer Sura Malaga of the SRM Design Group in Holmdel, New Jersey. "We wanted it to have a very understated look, yet have an elegant, castle-like style."

For the entry, a grand statement is made with the use of two types of Italian marble. The field of the floor consists of Botticino with a honed finish. Malaga

For this residence in New Jersey, the design goal was to create a look reminiscent of ancient Tuscany. This was done by combining stone with rich-looking maple and mahogany woods throughout. For the entry, a grand statement is made with the use of two types of Italian marble. The field of the floor consists of Botticino with a honed finish, while the accents are Giallo marble.

Throughout the rest of the home, Chinese slate is the predominant flooring material. The stone consists of shades of cream and gold—a lighter coloring than is typical of slate. The family room in the 12,000-square-foot residence has an open airy atmosphere—an effect accomplished by implementing large picture windows and the light-colored slate flooring. In this room, the stone flooring is comprised of 12 x 24-inch slate pieces laid in a running bond pattern.

Designer:
  **SRM Design Group,
  Holmdel, New Jersey**
Photos:
  Rosemary Carroll

explained that the muted look of the stone is a fitting expression of the Mediterranean style. The Botticino is complemented with smaller tiles of Giallo marble, which were used for a border. "We went to Italy and selected everything from the quarries there," said Malaga.

Throughout the rest of the home, Chinese slate is the predominant flooring material. Considering that the homeowners have a family of five boys, "slate evoked the rugged elegance desired by the homeowners," said Malaga. The stone consists of shades of cream and gold—a lighter coloring than is typical of slate.

The family room in the 12,000-square-foot residence has an open, airy atmosphere—an effect accomplished by implementing large picture windows and light-colored slate flooring. In this room, the stone flooring is comprised of 12 x 24-inch slate pieces laid in a running bond pattern.

The same stone is also used in the kitchen and dining areas, providing a connecting element between the two spaces. "We married the kitchen and family room with the slate," says Malaga, adding that the material was also carried out to the patio. "It's a very rugged, natural-looking stone."

In the kitchen, the material was laid in 6 x 24-inch pieces to create a herringbone pattern. The neutral tones of the slate contrast with the darker granite countertops and rich mahogany cabinetry. The granite, which features an ornate edge detail and intricate shaping at the corners, was also used for furnishings such as the china closet, further uniting the different spaces within the home. From start to finish, it took about a year and a half to complete construction of the house.

Below:

The granite countertops in the kitchen feature an ornate edge detail and intricate shaping at the corners. This stone was also used for furnishings such as the china closet, further uniting the different spaces within the home.

Opposite:

Chinese slate was also used for the kitchen and dining areas, providing a connecting element for the two spaces. Here, the material is laid in 6 x 24-inch pieces to create a herringbone pattern. The neutral tones of slate contrast with darker granite countertops and rich mahogany cabinetry.

Photos: **Rosemary Carroll**

Kitchen Spaces

When choosing stone for a kitchen space, homeowners are again faced with the question of how much color they want to use. While some designs enhance a kitchen space with bright, vibrant colors, others present a more subtle approach.

In any case, natural stone can be used for a broad range of applications in a kitchen, including flooring, countertops, backsplashes and center islands. Many times the stone selections are coordinated with other elements such as cabinetry and even appliances.

Remaining timeless

In her designs for residential kitchens, Barbara Karpf of Barbara H. Karpf Interiors, Inc., in New York chooses to use materials that transcend fashion trends. "I prefer to design with colors that are timeless," she states. "I like to use products that will hold up indefinitely. Things that work now should also work fifteen years from now."

In designing her own kitchen, Karpf desired a modern feel, one that would also acknowledge the history of the space. Since her New York City apartment was built in the 1920s, she chose to remain in touch with its linear themes. "I wanted to keep the architectural integrity of the apartment," comments Karpf. "I kept it linear to make a subtle reference to that."

Not dissimilar to many kitchens in Manhattan, the area is comprised of a fairly modest 9 x 13-foot space. "It is a typical galley kitchen, which can be

In a diverse combination of kitchen surfaces, this space combines honed white limestone flooring with ceramic tile for the backsplash, Brazilian granite for the countertops and sealed wood for the center island. The overall look of the space was conceived to recall the look of a French country kitchen, with carved pinewood for the oven hood, cabinetry and even the facing of the refrigerator.

Designer: **Gullans & Brooks Associates, Inc.**
Builder: **Stasio, Inc., Ridgefield, Connecticut**
Stone Supplier: **Fordham Marble, Stamford, Connecticut**

For this galley kitchen space in her New York apartment, Barbara H. Karpf chose a honed and tumbled White Carrara marble with a large-scale basket-weave pattern for the floor, which helped brighten the space. The White Carrara marble is utilized as 6 x 12-inch tiles, with 3 x 3-inch pieces of polished Vermont Verde Antique marble completing the basket-weave pattern. "The gray veining of the White Carrara marble does not show dirt as readily as an all-white stone, and because it is not slippery, it is also safe," said the designer. The kitchen countertops are slabs of polished Vermont Verde Antique marble.

Designer:
Barbara H. Karpf Interiors, Inc., New York, New York
Stone Suppliers:
American Stone & Supply Inc., New Rochelle, New York (White Carrara marble); Marble Modes, College Point, New York (Vermont Verde Antique marble)
Photo:
Davis A. Gaffga

tight," says Karpf. "Everything—down to where the cutlery would be placed—had to be thoroughly thought out to make the kitchen as spacious as possible."

In addition to opening up the kitchen by providing a specific placement for each item, Karpf was aware that the new stone she chose for the floor would also make a tremendous difference in the dark room. "I knew that I wanted the floor to be white, but with teenagers and dogs in residence, it also had to be functional," she said.

After some careful consideration, Karpf decided on honed and tumbled White Carrara marble with a large-scale basket-weave pattern for the floor. The White Carrara marble is utilized as 6 x 12-inch tiles, with 3 x 3-inch pieces of polished Vermont Verde Antique marble completing the basket-weave pattern. "The gray veining of the White Carrara marble does not show dirt as readily as an all-white stone, and because it is not slippery, it is also safe," comments the designer. "Also, since the pattern is larger than usual, it projects a real style," says Karpf, adding that a traditional-sized basket-weave pattern of the same stones can be found in the bathroom.

The kitchen countertops are slabs of polished Vermont Verde Antique marble. Again, Karpf decided to use this stone based on her experience with another design. "This particular marble is not only luxurious and velvety, but it is also sturdy enough for use in kitchens," she says.

Karpf then added a little more color to the kitchen by utilizing handmade tiles from Waterworks for the backsplash. She selected 6 x 6-inch tiles that feature twelve different hand-painted fruits, including a peach, an orange and grapes. In addition to these tiles, she also used handmade white field tiles that matched perfectly with the painted ones. "I wanted to give the backsplash a more modern look," she states. "I was able to do so by setting the tiles in a linear way, spacing the painted tiles three tiles apart from one another."

For the cabinets, Karpf used custom-made cabinet doors, which are identical to the other doors in the apartment. She also put in a plaster molding and tray ceiling and closed up a maid's-room door to create a U shape for the kitchen. "I wanted a kitchen that would be comfortable to walk around in, and the U shape provided that as well as a tremendous amount of serving space," reflects the designer. Because the marble was sealed, and is holding up nicely, the only maintenance needed is the regular use of a grout cleaner. "Not only is the kitchen functional, but it is also aesthetically pleasing," comments Karpf.

Remodeling with color

An example of how Karpf uses color in her designs can be seen in the renovation of Frost Mill Manor in Millneck, New York. Built in the 1920s and used as the Smithers Foundation for Alcohol Abuse as well as a residence for a brief period, the twenty-five-room mansion had been vacant for many years. Karpf was in charge of remodeling the kitchen. She opted to retrofit the 16 x 24-foot space, working with existing elements as well as adding her own ideas.

In this 16 x 24-foot kitchen space set within a 1920s residence, the design entails the use of a broad range of brightly colored elements, including yellow cabinetry, lively patterned fabrics around the windows, and deep red stools at the center island. As a neutral supplement to these elements, the yellow Formica countertops and backsplash were replaced with Hauteville Dore French limestone.

The designer knew that the kitchen would work well with a diverse color palette. "I pre-determined a pale yellow kitchen, but I also wanted to do an entire story in color," Karpf said. This design goal entailed the use of a broad range of brightly colored elements, including yellow cabinetry, lively patterned fabrics around the windows and deep red stools at the center island.

To ensure that the countertops would not take away from these surroundings, Karpf chose to replace the yellow Formica countertops and backsplash with French limestone. "The limestone provides a softer look than granite, and most clients ask for it," said the designer. "I also love the look of limestone as well as its versatility."

Hauteville Dore French limestone was selected for the countertops in the kitchen, and a hand-chiseled finish was chosen for the island countertop. The

limestone has a natural patina that also allows for easy cleaning, according to Karpf.

The utilization of the limestone, which has some red tones in it, worked well with her idea for a yellow kitchen. The designer explained that "Hauteville Dore is harmonious yet colorful," adding that she also revitalized the existing cabinetry in yellow and green. For the wall surfaces not

The use of French limestone, which has some red tones in it, worked well with the designer's plan for a colorful kitchen. For the wall surfaces not clad in limestone tiles, the designer specified *poudre de pierre,* a special plaster-and-ground-marble finish imported from France that resembles natural limestone.

Designer: **Barbara H. Karpf Interiors, Inc., New York, New York**
Stone Supplier: **Haifa, Inc., Lake Worth, Florida**
Photo: **Davis A. Gaffga**

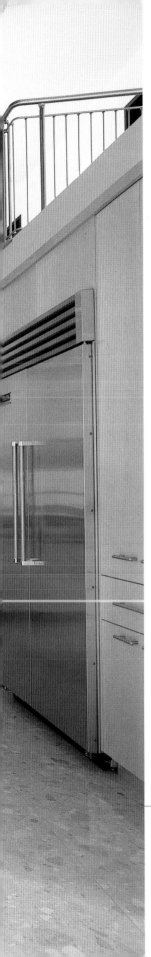

clad in limestone tiles, Karpf specified *poudre de pierre,* a special plaster-and-ground-marble finish imported from France that resembles natural limestone.

To complete the design, Karpf chose porcelain tiles for the floor in a style to resemble terra-cotta. "The Casali Cadel Bosco porcelain tiles look authentic and identical to terra-cotta," said Karpf. "The color also picked up the reds used in the kitchen."

Although the overall aesthetic and setting for the kitchen is somewhat traditional, it incorporates high-tech products alongside classic building materials. "I wanted it to be a functional residential kitchen, one that can work for a single person, a family or a catered event," said Karpf. Aiming to update the kitchen for the twenty-first century, the designer used modern appliances for the work and entertainment stations as well as a state-of-the-art cooking center and a media center.

A minimalist look

For a 12,000-square-foot residence in Colts Neck, New Jersey, designer Sura Malaga of SRM Design, Ltd., utilized a variety of stones to give the home a natural feel without being ornate. "We wanted a minimalist look," says Malaga, explaining that the primary objective was to give the home an unconstrained feel. In her design, a combination of limestone, marble, soapstone and marble agglomerate achieves this look.

The light-colored marble agglomerate is used as flooring throughout the kitchen space, contrasting with the green

A minimalist look was achieved in this kitchen space with the help of marble agglomerate flooring and green soapstone countertops. While the countertops were made from slabs, the floor is comprised of 18 x 18-inch tiles. "The agglomerate looks like a terrazzo floor," said Malaga. "It puts actual marble pieces together and gives a monochromatic natural look."

Designer: **SRM Design, Ltd., Holmdel, New Jersey**
Stone Suppliers: **Trans Ceramica, Philadelphia, Pennsylvania (limestone);**
Rover Inc., Cincinnati, Ohio (marble agglomerate)

soapstone countertops. While the countertops were made from slabs, the floor is comprised of 18 x 18-inch tiles. "The agglomerate looks like a terrazzo floor," comments Malaga. "It puts actual marble pieces together and gives a monochromatic, but natural look."

In addition to natural stone, a broad range of design elements continue the minimalist theme. The hanging light fixtures are intentionally understated, and the cabinetry, furnishings and appliances feature simple linear dimensions in light wood and stainless steel.

Malaga explains that her clients are often skeptical about using limestone in high-traffic areas, due to the fear of staining. She does her best to convince them that, with the proper sealer, there should be no worries. "Staining is the main concern with limestone," says Malaga, adding that another concern is water penetration (when used in bathroom applications). "If the walls and floors are sealed properly, it should be fine."

Throughout the two-and-a-half-year period when the house was being built, Malaga worked closely with the installer to ensure the stone was laid correctly. "I gave them a detailed plan and made field visits," she recalls. "Because of the clean line, we had to make sure that everything was monochromatic-looking. It was important to have the line straight. Because of the clean look, it had to be perfect."

In addition to natural stone, a broad range of design elements continue the minimalist theme. The hanging light fixtures are intentionally understated, and the cabinetry, furnishings and appliances feature simple linear dimensions in light wood and stainless steel.

Mixing it up

Of course, choosing stone for one kitchen element—such as the countertops—does not mean that all "hard surfaces" in the space have to be comprised of natural stone. Homeowners who are seeking more variety in their materials palette have found that natural stone and ceramic tile can be an ideal combination in a kitchen environment.

In most instances where stone and ceramics are combined, the durability of a natural-stone countertop is matched with the uniform color tones of ceramic tile for the floors, backsplash and other vertical surfaces. By using stone for the countertops—the most demanding application in a kitchen space—the overall durability factor is high, and the materials palette is diversified.

This was the case for a residence designed by Calder Interiors, which utilizes Carrara White marble for the kitchen countertops and Lilac marble for the center island, which also features a wet bar. The natural-stone counters contrast with a classic ceramic mosaic pattern on the floor, which continues from the kitchen into the breakfast nook. The table within the breakfast nook, finished with a Carrara White tabletop, also ties into the design scheme.

Reversing this motif for another residence, Calder Interiors selected honed Noce travertine for the kitchen flooring, with black ceramic tile topping the

This residence utilizes Carrara White marble for the kitchen countertops and Lilac marble for the center island, which also features a wet bar. The natural-stone counters contrast with a classic ceramic-mosaic pattern in the floors.

The ceramic mosaic pattern continues into the breakfast nook, where the table is furnished with a Carrara White tabletop.

Designer:
**Calder Interiors,
New York, New York**

center island. In this case, the homeowners were willing to sacrifice a small measure of durability in order to achieve the desired aesthetic. Although ceramic tile itself is quite durable for a kitchen environment, overall maintenance can be more of a factor due to the grout lines, which must be kept clean to preserve the proper look.

In an even more diverse combination of kitchen surfaces, in one home Gullans & Brooks Associates, Inc., combined honed white limestone flooring with ceramic tile for the backsplash, Brazilian granite for the countertops and sealed wood for the center island (see page 69).

The overall look of the space was conceived to recall the look of a French country kitchen, with carved pine wood for the oven hood, cabinetry, and even the refrigerator. This is enhanced by the neutral tones of the flooring, which is

In this kitchen area, the honed Noce travertine flooring is contrasted with black ceramic tile for the center island top. In this case, the homeowners were willing to sacrifice a small measure of durability in order to achieve the desired aesthetic.

Although ceramic tile itself is quite durable for a kitchen environment, overall maintenance can be more of a factor due to the grout lines, which must be kept clean to preserve the proper look.

Designer:
  **Calder Interiors,
  New York, New York**

comprised of 18 x 12-inch limestone tiles installed in a running bond pattern.

But a true blending of materials is found in the countertops and backsplash. The room's focal point, a large center island/breakfast bar, is topped with pine wood. The warm tones of the pine are complemented by the golden hue of the Giallo Veneziano granite countertops, which were quarried in Brazil. The design scheme is completed with the use of rectangular ceramic tiles in a nonintrusive off-white tone for the backsplash.

In the kitchen below, the flooring is comprised of 18 x 12-inch limestone tiles installed in a running bond pattern. The warm tones of the pine are well complemented by the golden hue of the Giallo Veneziano granite countertops, which were quarried in Brazil. The design scheme is complete with the use of rectangular ceramic tiles for the backsplash in an nonintrusive off-white tone.

This kitchen space contrasts contemporary styling with rustic elements. Modern light fixtures hang from the exposed wooden trusses, and the walls are ceramic tile in a brick-like pattern. The flooring is comprised of textured slate in a geometric pattern of multiple-sized tiles. The stone for the countertop, backsplash and center island—referred to as Charcoal granite—combines the color tones that can be found throughout the kitchen.

Designer: **Connie L. Gustafson, CKD, Sawhill Custom Kitchens & Designs, Inc., Minneapolis, Minnesota**
Photo: **Andrew Bordwin**

Verde Maritaka granite, selected primarily for its durability, was employed for the countertops and backsplash in this new kitchen design.

Stone Supplier: **National Stone Drafting, Denver, Colorado**

Dark beige travertine is the feature element of this cooking area. On the walls, the stone is used as 4 x 4-inch tiles with insets of decorative ceramic tiles. Meanwhile, the floor pattern combines the travertine with Carrara White and Tropical Brown marble. Carrara White was also used for the kitchen countertops.

Stone Supplier: **Connecticut Stone Supplies, Milford, Connecticut**

Above:

In this kitchen, Jerusalem Gold limestone was employed around the cooking area. A decorative floor insert features a Roman mosaic with a rope border and a Florentine drop-in of limestone and travertine tesserae. The backsplash is Cerde St. Nicolaus travertine, and the floor tile in the field is a glazed ceramic tile.

Stone Supplier: **Country Floors, Los Angeles, California**

Left:

A combination of darker stone materials was chosen for this kitchen space, including Durango Stone™, a marble product from Mexico, for the floors and a Juparana granite for the countertops. The dark tones of the stonework are offset by high ceilings and ample natural light flowing in from outdoors. The counters feature an intricate edge detail and ornate corners to add visual interest, and different shades of Durango Stone were used to form a border around the space.

Stone Supplier: **World Wide Stone Corp., Phoenix, Arizona**

An elliptical contrast

The effect of stone on a kitchen space is achieved not only through the use of color and texture but also by the shape of the counters and the edgework. For a kitchen space in northern California, the clean linear patterns are subtly contrasted with the Mint Green stone countertops.

The homeowners and the designer, Gerald Jacobs, AIA, of San Rafael, California, wanted to achieve a modern look. This was achieved through the use of simple cabinetry and unadorned stainless-steel appliances and fixtures. Continuing the understated pattern, the countertops feature a soft pastel tone with subtle veining.

Variety was added through the detailing of the countertops, which have a full bullnosed edge wherein all of the edgework is completely rounded. Additionally, the stone top at the breakfast bar terminates in a half-circle, providing aesthetic appeal as well as safety (by eliminating the protruding square corner). The entire counter is supported by a single brass pole, introducing yet another complementary element to the space. "I wanted consistency, and the most dramatic part of this is the stone," says Jacobs.

For this kitchen space in northern California, the clean linear patterns are subtly contrasted with the Mint Green stone countertops. The homeowners desired to achieve a modern look for the space, which was achieved through the use of simple cabinetry and unadorned appliances and fixtures in stainless steel.

Variety was added through the detailing of the countertops, which was specified with a full bullnose edge, wherein all of the edgework is completely rounded.

The stone top at the breakfast bar terminates in a half-circle, providing aesthetic appeal. The entire counter is supported by a single brass pole, introducing yet another complementary element to the space.

Designer:
Gerald Jacobs, AIA,
San Rafael, California

Two different varieties of natural stone were used for this kitchen space. Honey travertine was used for the countertops, fabricated to allow for an undermounted sink. Walls were covered with 4 x 4-inch tumbled Botticino marble tile.

Bathroom Spaces

When choosing natural stone for a bathroom application, homeowners are offered a wide range of possibilities. Contemporary and classic designs are utilizing natural stone for virtually all the elements in a bathroom space, including the vanity tops, shower stalls, tub surrounds and, of course, the floors.

From a purely functional point of view, the use of stone in a bathroom offers a higher level of durability and resistance to water damage than virtually any other product. From an aesthetic standpoint, homeowners are bringing natural stone into bathroom spaces to create a haven where they can retreat from the stresses of everyday life. Stone is often used to highlight an area of the bathroom such as a steam shower or Jacuzzi tub, elevating the visual presence of these amenities.

Opposite: **For this bathroom space in the Hollywood Hills of California, the homeowners wanted a design that would reflect the natural feel of the nearby state park. To echo California earth tones, Autumn Mist slate was chosen for the bathroom flooring, shower and Jacuzzi tub surround.**

Above: **A platform tub built up to window level is surrounded by tile that includes a decorative border frieze. The ornately patterned wallpaper, along with the curvature of the tub, though perfectly modern, give a slight nod to Victorian styling.**

Designer: **Arch-Interiors Design Group, Inc., Beverly Hills, California**
Stone Supplier: **Southland Stone, North Hollywood, California (slate)**
Photo: **Glenn Daidone**

Contractor: **Cameo Homes, Salt Lake City, Utah**
Stone Supplier: **Contempo Tile, Salt Lake City, Utah**
Photo: **Kurt Wahlner**

A neutral palette

While Christopher Grubb of Arch-Interiors Design Group, Inc., in Beverly Hills, California, believes that color plays a role in stone selection, he also finds that neutral materials are more prevalent in bathrooms. "Each client is different, and each design has to be done according to the client's wishes," states Grubb. However, the use of natural stone, such as slate and granite, is a common thread throughout many of the bathrooms done by Arch-Interiors.

In one bathroom, located in the Hollywood Hills of California, the clients' 3,000-square-foot residence is situated close to a state park, and the homeowners wanted a bathroom design that would reflect the surrounding environment. They also desired an abundance of natural light and a space that would feel open. "The clients were very much into California earth tones," comments Grubb.

For the vanity top, make-up counter and bench in the shower, Grubb selected Golden Sunset granite to complement the slate.

Opposite:

Autumn Mist slate is utilized as 12 x 12-inch tiles, which are arranged in a 45-degree running bond pattern on the floor and are set on the diagonal for the Jacuzzi tub.

Photos: **Glenn Daidone**

In providing this earthy look, Arch-Interiors chose Autumn Mist slate for the bathroom flooring, shower and Jacuzzi tub surround. "The clients wanted to reflect other finishes in the house," says Grubb. "It was important that this room relate to the whole house. For them, this material was just right, and they found the variation in the stone fascinating." The stone was utilized as 12 x 12-inch slate tiles, which were arranged in a 45-degree running bond pattern on the floor. For the vanity top, makeup counter and bench in the shower, Grubb selected Golden Sunset granite to provide a complementary element to the slate. "The

In this bathroom, the wife wanted a touch of Hawaiian/Asian influence, while the husband leaned towards a more contemporary look. Rustic Yellow slate was already in place elsewhere in the house and satisfied both needs in the bathroom as well. A sunken steam shower is the focal point of the bathroom, with slate walls, granite niches, a granite bench and dual showerheads.

Golden Leaf granite was also employed for the vanity tops, complemented by rich-toned woodwork.

Designer: **Arch-Interiors Design Group, Inc., Beverly Hills, California**
Stone Supplier: **Walker Zanger, Sylmar, California; Stone Resources, (granite)**
Photos: **Steve Pomerants**

color palette and blend of materials came together very quickly," notes Grubb.

For another residence, also located in the Hollywood Hills, the goals were a bit different. "The bathroom was the one area of the house that had not yet been redone," says Grubb. "The clients wanted to combine the existing workout room and bathroom and make it one master suite."

As a couple, the clients had unique tastes. While the wife wanted a touch of Hawaiian/Asian influence, the husband leaned toward a more contemporary look. Rustic Yellow slate was already in place elsewhere in the house, and, because of its Asian look and contemporary feel, it was selected again for use in the bathroom.

"It was not exactly the same color slate as other areas of the house, but it had a variation of all the colors they love," comments Grubb. The 18 x 18-inch tiles were set on the floor at 45-degree angles to minimize grout lines and emphasize the room's size. Other materials used included polished Golden Leaf granite, which was employed for horizontal surfaces such as the vanity tops, the shower bench, and the shower niche and tub surround. Arch-Interiors also employed rich-toned woodwork for the vertical surfaces of the vanity and glass surrounds, and the glass features a pressed pattern to provide privacy.

The sunken steam shower is the focal point of the bathroom, with slate walls, granite niches, a granite bench, and dual showerheads. Slate walls also surround the tub area, and the Jacuzzi tub surround was carefully detailed to appear as though it was carved from a single block of granite.

Comfort details, such as the shower-stall niche, were carved from granite.

The third bathroom, in a home located in the Los Angeles area, needed to be opened up from its confined 80-square-foot space. In this project, the client was quite active in determining the final design. As a frequent traveler, the home-owner enjoyed the luxury of hotels and wanted to achieve the same ambience in his own bathroom. "The client had done most of the necessary research, and had a good feel for the colors and material he wanted," says Grubb. "We simply fine-tuned them by positioning the materials appropriately."

For this bathroom space, large slabs of onyx were selected for the walls and floors, with more detailed pieces for the moldings and tub surround and facing.

Stone Supplier: **Haifa, Inc., Lake Worth, Florida**

With thoughtful use of natural slate, this bathroom design in the Los Angeles area opens a confined 80-square-foot space with a door to the outside. The homeowner wanted to achieve the feeling of a luxury hotel.

The floor and walls employ 12 x 12-inch Jade Green slate set on the diagonal, with a 4-inch Absolute Black granite border.

To hold its own against the strong coloring of the slate, the material for the vanity needed to be substantial but scaled small enough not to encroach on the limited space. In response, a matte-green stone countertop was created as a simple rectangle with a 1½-inch backsplash.

Designer: **Arch-Interiors Design Group, Inc., Beverly Hills, California**
Stone Supplier: **Bourget Brothers, Santa Monica, California**
Photos: **Ken Chen Photography**

The design team transformed the shower stall into a seamless glass steam shower. They employed 12 x 12-inch Jade Green slate on the floor and walls, set on the diagonal, with a 4-inch Absolute Black granite border. Because of the strong coloring of the slate, the material for the vanity needed to be substantial enough to coordinate with the walls and floors, but scaled down enough so that it did not encroach on the limited space. As a result, a matte-green stone counter-top was created as a simple rectangle with a $1^1/2$-inch backsplash.

Because there are some hard-water concerns in California, Grubb notes the importance of maintaining the slate. "It was originally sealed two or three times, but it still has to be kept very clean, and I recommend that it be resealed once a year," he comments.

The stones used in all three of Arch-Interiors' projects were given a honed finish to provide the more natural look desired by the clients. "When slate is put on vertical surfaces, it really envelops the client in the product," notes Grubb. "Clients are very much drawn to slate for its naturalness and beauty, and they are drawn to granite for its exciting color and texture."

Capturing 1920s style

Designed as a showcase home to benefit the Los Angeles Philharmonic, a private residence in Pasadena, California, makes extensive use of stone in the bathroom. The administrators of the show house selected Gene Zettle Interiors in Pasadena to design both his and hers master bathrooms. "We were able to select the color palette, and we wanted to create bathrooms that looked as though they had been there since the house was built in the 1920s," says designer Gene Zettle.

For the woman's bathroom, Zettle chose Dore Royale and Giallo Antico Antique marble for the floor, and Opus Anticato, Verde Luna, and Murgiano marble for the walls. "We had color palettes we were trying to deal with, and these stones worked well," notes Zettle. "The marble added a little more texture."

The floor uses 18 x 18-inch tiles of Dore Royale and Giallo Antico Antique marble, forming a checkerboard pattern, and the stones were alternately honed and etched. "This lends an air of antiquity to the stone and creates different textures and colors to produce a checkerboard effect," comments Zettle. The wainscot on the wall is a standard mosaic pattern, echoing the floor design. "Mosaics

Opposite:

For this woman's bathroom in Pasadena, California, part of a show house originally constructed in the 1920s, the design intent was to create a space that looked like it had always been there. The materials palette uses Dore Royale and Giallo Antico Antique marble for the floor, and Opus Anticato, Verde Luna and Murgiano marble for the walls.

Designer:
**Gene Zettle Interiors,
Pasadena, California**
Stone Supplier:
**Walker Zanger,
Sylmar, California**

are very suitable for homes with an old-world Italian look," says Zettle. "The wainscoting repeats what is on the floor at a much smaller scale." Because the wainscot is used around the tub area, it was honed to protect it from water.

To complete this antique look, moldings were added above the wainscot and a Pullman cabinet was designed with a custom, old-world painted finish. "We created the architectural detailing to look as if it was

The wainscot on the wall is a standard mosaic pattern, which echoes the floor design; a mosaic border runs throughout the space.

always there," said Zettle. "We also designed a dressing table to look like it came out of the 1920s."

Textured stone materials were also used in the man's bathroom, but a different color palette was selected. "In the woman's we used green and cream, and in the man's we used stronger gold and russet colors," states Zettle. Mosaic pieces of rust-colored marble were used for the shower base and bench, with larger gold tiles set on the diagonal for the shower walls and floor.

In addition to the coloration, the texture of the stone helped achieve the design goal for the bathrooms. "The material was also chosen because the stones had an aged look," says Zettle. "I wanted to keep the design consistent with the original architectural intent of the house instead of giving it a foreign look."

The man's room features strong colors such as gold and russet. Mosaic pieces of rust-colored marble were used for the shower base and bench, with larger gold tiles set on the diagonal for the shower walls and floor.

A textured space

In San Jose, California, three different varieties of stone—including limestone and tumbled marble—were selected to provide the right color palette and texture for a bathroom. "I wanted to create a neutral, yet textural space—a subtle, but very rich environment," explains designer Alison Whittaker of Alison Whittaker Design in Los Gatos, California, who adds that she initially needed to convince the homeowners of the practicality of the material.

The shower in this Pasadena house was designed with a combination of limestone and tumbled marble. The space features a carved molding of gray limestone and an intricately cut leaf pattern that combines both varieties of limestone.

In this bathroom application, 12 x 12-inch limestone tiles in beige and gray tones were used for the flooring. The tiles were set on the diagonal, with 4 x 4-inch tumbled marble tiles interspersed into the pattern as an accent.

A featured element in the bathroom is the raised tub, which is surrounded by windows on three sides. The front of the tub is faced with cherry wood, with gray limestone used in slab form for the tub surround and steps. A border of tumbled marble frames the entire tub as well as the flooring where it meets the walls and shower.

The shower stall was also designed with the same combination of limestone and tumbled marble. Additionally, the shower features a carved molding of gray limestone and an intricately cut leaf pattern that combines two varieties of limestone.

In San Jose, California, three different varieties of stone, including limestone and tumbled marble, were selected to provide the right color palette and texture for a bathroom space. For the flooring, 12 x 12-inch limestone tiles in beige and gray tones were set on the diagonal, with 4 x 4-inch tumbled marble tiles interspersed into the pattern as an accent.

Designer: **Alison Whittaker Design, Los Gatos, California**
Stone Supplier: **Walker Zanger, Sylmar, California**

Contemporary Design

Part of the current appeal of natural stone is its suitability for the "back to basics" movement in residential design. This movement is a departure from the more high-tech approach of years past toward living spaces simplified and softened through natural materials. And despite the elegance of natural stone, homeowners are finding uses for the material that are more understated. They are realizing that more isn't always better. There are ways to incorporate natural stone into interior designs without making a bold statement. Tumbled or honed stones lend themselves to these types of contemporary designs.

Combining stone with other building materials such as tile and wood opens the doors for endless design possibilities and allows for stone to be introduced into a home without being overdone.

It appears that when it comes to natural stone, many owners of today's high-end homes are opting for a more subdued color scheme in interior designs as well. Although splashes of color are evident in accents and detailing, a significant portion of residential designs in natural stone today include light colors and softer tones.

"Certainly during the 1980s, the focus was on very shiny, hard materials," said Mary Douglas Drysdale, founder of Drysdale Design Associates, which has offices in Washington, D.C., and New York. "As the eighties ended and the nineties began, I think there was a real turning away from that sort of look, and

"Casual elegance" were the watchwords in the interior design of this southern California home. An open plan, soft desert colors, special lighting and large windows harmonize with the patterns of marble, slate floors and abstract paintings.

Developer/Contractor: **Foxx Homes, Palm Desert, California**
Architect: **Dave Prest, Palm Desert, California**
Interior Designer: **William Miller Design, Palm Desert, California**
Stone Supplier: **Moreno Tile, Cathedral City, California (slate floors)**
Photo: **Kurt Wahlner**

the materials I see clients wanting now have a much more natural quality."

Catering to the high-end residential market, Drysdale said her savvy clientele expects a high level of detail and sophisticated finishes, including natural stone. They represent many of today's homeowners who have cultivated an interest in all aspects of design through traveling, reading architecture and fashion magazines, and just keeping up with their neighbors, many of whom seem to have embraced stone as a "must-have" element in their homes.

For this penthouse in Washington, D.C., French limestone composes the flooring in the dining room, where a solid maple table is distinguished by a green marble inlay. Catering to the high-end residential market, designer Mary Douglas Drysdale said her savvy clientele expects a high level of detail and sophisticated finishes, including natural stone.

The fireplace surround and mantel in the penthouse are comprised of simple pieces of French limestone to blend with the neutral tones, which are prevalent throughout the living space.

"It's interesting. I've been in business for approximately twenty years, and during that period of time it seems that the American public has either rediscovered or fallen in love with interior stone," comments Drysdale. "I think it began with a rediscovery of marble in the entry foyer, and from there it certainly has grown. Even fifteen years ago, I think it was considered a luxury to find marble or granite in the bathroom and/or kitchen, and today that's almost an expectation."

For a penthouse in Washington, D.C., the designer combined natural stone floors and neutral-painted walls with touches of vibrant color to create an introspective contrast. The flooring throughout the living and dining areas is comprised of French limestone, which features the warm tone and subtle veining pattern that was aesthetically desired, but has the durability needed for a high-traffic flooring application. Natural stone was also used for functional elements such as the dining room table, which features a green marble inlay within a surface of

In the kitchen area, Drysdale selected a stark color palette of solid white cabinetry, appliances and walls, accented by salt-and-pepper granite for the floors and backsplash. Natural stone provided the technical and visual characteristics specific to the space.

Designer:
**Mary Douglas Drysdale,
Washington, D.C./
New York, New York**

solid maple wood, as well as the fireplace surround and mantel, which are comprised of simple pieces of French limestone.

In the kitchen area, Drysdale selected a stark color palette of solid white cabinetry, appliances and walls, accented with salt-and-pepper granite on the floors and backsplash. Meanwhile, the countertops are comprised of man-made solid surface material with an off-white tone to further enhance the overall design scheme.

Using stone throughout

Homeowners are just as concerned with the resilience of building materials as they are with their aesthetic appeal. For a residence in High Point, North Carolina, the homeowners planned on using only granite for the countertops. After a visit to a local showroom, however, they reconsidered their options.

"The homeowners came in and showed me the layout of the house," says Len Malavé of Granite & Marble by Malavé in Greensboro, North Carolina. "All they were going to do in stone was the kitchen, and they came in for a kitchen countertop." Before they left, the homeowners decided to include marble and granite flooring and slab showers in addition to their plans for the kitchen. In fact, they opted to use stone in every room of the house and on the exterior as well.

"The majority of the stone was selected for its durability," comments Malavé. "The color and composition—whether marble or granite—was also taken into consideration."

The inlay in the entranceway was made on-site and consists of Tazmanian Gold marble and Black Absolute granite within a field of Crema Marfil marble. According to Malavé, the three-dimensional effect of the design was a slight variation of an inlay created for another project that the homeowners had admired.

The use of Crema Marfil was continued through the foyer and down the hall, creating an open space in a classic color scheme. Diamond accents in Black Absolute were added to the stair treads to differentiate them from the rest of the Crema Marfil marble flooring.

Crema Marfil was employed in other areas of the home, including the master suite. "The homeowners were aiming to make the house open and airy, so they stuck with a lot of neutral colors," Malavé notes, adding that his clients favored the light tones

Designer:
Willard Stewart, High Point, North Carolina
Stone Supplier/
Fabricator/Installer:
Granite & Marble by Malavé, Greensboro, North Carolina
Photos:
David Sean Lorczak

The inlay in the entranceway of this High Point, North Carolina, residence consists of Tazmanian Gold marble and Black Absolute granite within a field of Crema Marfil marble—all of which were cut on-site. The use of Crema Marfil continues through the foyer and down the hall, creating an open space in a classic color scheme. To further add to the elegance of the space, diamond accents in Black Absolute were inserted in the stair treads to set off the Crema Marfil marble flooring.

Similar to "her" master bath in the house, "his" master bath has a Karma tile floor with a Black Absolute granite border and diamond accents to echo the pattern of colors in the wallpaper and mirror frame.

of the material. The Crema Marfil floor in the master suite's sitting room was laid out using 18 x 18-inch tiles in a simple grid pattern.

The powder room features a carved sink in Crema Marfil, as well as a full-sheet slab wall of the same marble. Rooms such as this are what diversified the project, explains Malavé, since they used both tiles and slabs.

The most important detail of these installations is the bookmatching, where-in two slabs cut from the same block of stone are laid in a manner that empha-sizes the similar veining patterns. "We always bookmatch the slabs, as can be seen in the showers," says Malavé. "We cut the slabs so the veining runs together when it is installed. You can barely see the seams."

The bookmatching is also visible in the columns surrounding the Jacuzzi tub in the "hers" master bath. This room also features Karma stone from Greece, which was used for the countertop, flooring, tub surround, stairs, and columns. Even the decorative urns are carved from this stone. The Absolute Black tile inlay on the floor was added to complement the black frame of the mirror.

A black mirror is also an important fixture in the "his" master bath. The inlaid floor has a black border and black accents to match the black in the mir-ror's frame and the wallpaper, similar to that of the "hers" master bath.

Adding a bit of spice to the décor and the continuous neutral colors, Rojo Alicante marble was selected for the countertop in the spare bathroom. The red tones are highlighted with light-colored veining, which complements the use of Crema Marfil on the floor.

Crema Marfil was again employed for the floor in the combination kitchen and den area, allowing for a unifying theme throughout the entire house, Malavé explains. The pattern of diamond accents in the flooring is also continued throughout the house, with Black Absolute diamonds breaking up the monotony of a single-color tile floor. In addition to the Crema Marfil, Luna Pearl granite was added to the décor of this area, used for the kitchen countertops as well as the bar top (both finished with half-bullnose edging).

One unique room in the house is the piano room. Used only to hold the piano, this room showcases a fitting musical theme. A border of "piano keys" made of Black Absolute granite and Thassos White marble runs around the perimeter of the room. The piano keys of this border are proportionately sized

Opposite:

"Her" master bath was a diverse installation job that utilized Karma tiles, slabs and blocks. The columns and the tub sur-round illustrate the book-matching technique, which involves matching the veining of the stone. The urns were carved from Karma stone as well.

Photos:
David Sean Lorczak

and raised off the floor to resemble actual piano keys. "Those who don't know ahead of time might even mistake them for the real thing," Malavé jokes.

A neutral palette

Designer Jennifer Biggs also favors a neutral-color palette when developing designs for upscale private residences. Such was the case for one particular home in Oak Ridge, North Carolina, where subdued shades of natural stone were combined with other materials to give the residence an elegant look with a European flair. The variety of stone not only enhanced the beauty of the home but also provided the strength and durability that a family with small children requires.

Marble accenting is obvious throughout the kitchen and den of this Oak Ridge, North Carolina, home. Combined with other neutral materials, the stone helps to complete the contemporary look of the residence.

To make the rooms in the house more open and airy, the neutral cream color was continued throughout the master suite.

Generating a touch of warmth in the room, the fireplace hearth and surround was carved from Indiana limestone.

Designer:
Jennifer Biggs, Oak Ridge, North Carolina
Stone Supplier/ Fabricator/Installer:
Granite & Marble by Malavé, Greensboro, North Carolina
Photos:
David Sean Lorczak

Illustrating how a little stone in a room can add to the décor, the designer chose Black Impala granite for the fireplace surround to accent the white painted mantel.

Using natural stone for furniture tops offers another way to add elegance to a room. The edging on this dresser is a double bullnose on a 1¼-inch-thick piece of Emperador marble.

Photos:
David Sean Lorczak

"Typically, I go in and choose everything because they like my style," says Biggs. "Most of my clients know that vibrant colors aren't me. Most of the time they turn me loose and let me do my thing."

For the 5,000-square-foot residence, the homeowners had a good idea of what style they desired. "They pretty much wanted a European, very traditional, classical look," comments the designer. "They wanted it to be livable, but also something that could be used for entertaining."

One way Biggs met the design objective was by creating a spacious kitchen area with large countertops made of Ubatuba granite from Brazil with a highly detailed "triple waterfall" edge. The ornate countertops were fabricated with numerically controlled computer technology, and the granite was chosen for its color versatility. "I liked the color," she says. "It was deep and rich." She further explains that various tones could be pulled from the material and used as accents. "I didn't want a light stone, but I wanted something neutral. I don't like to use a whole lot of colors," says Biggs. "I don't want to date the house."

White wooden cabinetry and a wood floor were also used to complement the granite countertops. "In the kitchen, the Ubatuba was more the focal point and the paint was the background," comments Biggs, adding that marbleized columns were also included in the design.

Ubatuba granite was also used for the bar top that is found upstairs. Besides

being selected for aesthetic reasons, the material was also a practical choice, according to the designer. "You don't have to worry about scorching or scratching granite," she explains.

Moving into the living room, Black Impala granite with a polished finish was employed for the fireplace surround. "There were a lot of neutral tones, and I wanted to use the black because you can accessorize a lot with it," says Biggs. The dark granite added a contrast to the white-painted mantel.

Another use of stone that added to the elegance of the residence was in the furniture, purchased from a local furniture store. Tops made from Emperador marble were custom-cut to fit such furniture as dressers and tables. In the bedroom, the dresser has a double-bullnose edge with a thickness of $1^{1}/_{4}$ inches, while the buffet top was given a flat polished edge.

In the kitchen of the house, Ubatuba granite countertops were designed to be the focal point of the room. The stonework is complemented by white wooden cabinetry and a wood floor, as well as marbleized columns.

Simple elegance

For those who have a desire to use natural stone in the majority of an interior, but don't want to run the risk of looking too lavish, there are ways to make it work. It just requires the appropriate materials and a skilled eye.

One Manhattan apartment offers some insight into how this can be achieved. A full spectrum of stone has been incorporated into this residential design, but in a way that gives it simple elegance. The design includes limestone and marble in a range of sizes and finishes, from large polished tiles to small tumbled mosaic pieces. And the effect of these stones varies throughout the residence, depending on the room.

In this Manhattan apartment, perhaps the most striking use of stone can be found in the living room, where massive pieces of honed Chassagne Beige French limestone compose the fireplace wall and hearth.

The kitchen floor is comprised of 6 x 6-inch pieces of antique Beaumaniere Ramage limestone, with an accent border of 2 x 2-inch pieces of Jaunc Rose limestone.

Stone Supplier:
Walker Zanger,
Sylmar, California
Installer:
Jan Tile,
New Rochelle, New York
Photos:
William Hubbel

Perhaps the most striking use of stone can be found in the living room, where massive pieces of French limestone compose the fireplace wall and hearth. French limestone was also used for the kitchen floor, which is comprised of 6 x 6-inch pieces of antiqued Beaumaniere Ramage limestone with an accent border of 2 x 2-inch pieces of Jaunc Rose limestone. Helidoro limestone, employed in $1^{1}/4$-inch slabs, comprises the kitchen countertops.

The bathrooms also make extensive use of stone tiles and moldings, but the overall design illustrates how stone can be used extensively without looking ostentatious. The subtle details and comfortable feel of the stone design provide distinction without being overdone.

The master-bathroom shower floor is a single piece of honed Sahara Brown marble, while 12 x 12-inch tiles of polished Sahara Brown clad the rear wall to the ceiling, and the other walls to waist-high. The remaining wall spaces are covered with an antiqued mosaic border of Biancone and Tufo limestone.

Unconventional in nature

Whether the homeowners are sitting on the outdoor patio or resting on an indoor sofa, a private residence in Arizona projects a cool, relaxing image with its use of Ancient Tumbled Durango limestone from Mexico. Employed throughout the interior and exterior of the residence, the material's hues of beige and cream reflect the color palette of southwestern design style.

The homeowners selected the limestone because they were seeking an unconventional look that they believed the material could provide. The limestone was implemented for showers, tubs, a vanity top, and circular fireplace, as well as for both indoor and outdoor flooring.

"I really liked the Mediterranean tumbled look of the stone, which is thick, rich and durable," says builder Wade Cline of Cline's Custom Tile in Phoenix. "I also liked the color variations and the rough edges because it adds character."

The builder explains that the limestone was actually tumbled rather than acid-washed. "We wanted the floor to stay uniform," says Cline. More than 12,000 square feet of Durango stone was used for the project—most of which was used to lay the floor and outdoor patio as one continuous unit. "The outside patio flows around three sides of the house, and the indoor floor pattern is followed right out the doors and onto it," says Cline. "Standard pieces of stone were used throughout the home, except for raised areas such as the entryway, where cuts had to be custom-made in order for the pieces to fit correctly."

The floor consists of tiles in sizes of 16 x 16, 8 x 16 and 8 x 8 inches, which form a random, undetectable pattern. "You don't see the pattern, just broken up joints with no uniformity," said Cline. "In an installation done in the olden days you would see random cuts, but because today we need to know how much stone

Ancient Tumbled Durango limestone was used for both interior and exterior applications throughout this private residence in Fountain Hills, Arizona. A focal point of the great room is a large circular fireplace constructed entirely of limestone.

With a 3-inch-thick ledge created with 21-inch-long pieces, each piece is 9 inches wide on one side and 16 inches wide on the other.

The flooring of the Arizona residence consists of 16 x 16-, 8 x 8-, and 8 x 16-inch pieces of limestone, which create a broken-up floor with an undetectable pattern.

Designer/Installer:
Cline's Custom Tile, Phoenix, Arizona
Stone Supplier:
World Wide Stone Corp., Phoenix, Arizona
Photos:
Paul E. Loven/ Photographic Design

to order in advance, we had to stick to a pattern." The stone is installed directly to the slab using a thin-set method, which is standard for a slab installation; according to the designer it also provides a long-lasting bond.

The tumbled limestone was also incorporated in other areas of the home, such as the bathrooms, where 4 x 4-inch pieces were used for the showers, tubs and countertops. Additionally, an eight-foot circular fireplace was built in the living room with a three-inch-thick ledge and pieces that are twenty-one inches long. Each piece is nine inches wide on one side and sixteen inches wide on the other.

Installing the stonework took approximately six weeks to complete. A month later, the workers returned and installed the outside patio, which took an additional two weeks. The stone was finished with a penetrating sealer and then coated with a stone enhancer to further bring out the natural coloring of the material.

Despite the large size of the residence, the design was planned to provide a relaxed environment, according to the builder. "You would think with a house that big there would be an echo," comments Cline. "But there is no echo. The house has a very comfortable, warm atmosphere." Furthermore, the size of the project did not hinder the process. "There were no real challenges," says Cline. "It was a big job to coordinate, but it was made easy by a good product."

More than 12,000 feet of Durango Stone™ was used to furnish the project—most of which was used to lay the floor and outdoor patio as one continuous unit. The outside patio flows around three sides of the house, with the indoor floor pattern following through the doors to join the outside.

Photo: **Paul E. Loven/Photographic Design**

The use of stone materials in this contemporary design in the southern California desert shows the wide-ranging possibilities designers and architects are realizing in projects both large and small. The visitor to the house passes through a front yard berm of sand, local boulders and drought-resistant plantings. The berms are held in place with retaining walls covered with a stacked veneer of sandstone.

Overleaf:

Inside the house, the feeling is open, emphasized by the large expanse of "Earth" slate from Moreno Tile. The design concept of the space was referred to as "sophisticated contemporary, with ethnic accents," dictating the use of ceramics, wall hangings, the slate flooring and asymmetrical massing of the kitchen cabinets.

Developer/Contractor: **Foxx Homes, Palm Desert, California**
Architect: **Dave Prest, Palm Desert, California**
Interior Designer: **William Miller Design, Palm Desert, California**
Stone Supplier: **Eagle Marble & Granite, Los Angeles (interior stone)**
Photos: **Kurt Wahlner**

In the living room, the slate flooring stops and a custom-designed salt-and-pepper area rug takes over, complementing the polished Desert Brown granite fireplace. Although the wall behind the fireplace looks as though it too, were stone, it is actually a *faux* painting with raised horizontal bands.

The powder room off the entrance is a darker space illuminated by glass blocks punched through the exterior wall. The Earth slate runs right under the floating counter, elegantly covered with a countertop and backsplash of polished Black Galaxy granite, surmounted by a stainless steel "Timpani" basin from Kohler.

The kitchen layout is simplicity itself: one long counter on the right, and a serving island on the left. Both are topped with Juperano Fantastico granite. The faucet is a Price Pfister "Contempra."

Below is the formal dining area. It is made more spacious through the use of the wall-hung buffet, custom built for the house and topped in the same polished Desert Brown granite as the living room fireplace. The gravity-defying marble wall hanging is by Laddie John Dill.

In the master bedroom, the nightstands are covered in massive, thick-looking Noche Light honed travertine. Everything else in the room is fabric of some kind.

The Noche Light honed travertine is also used in most of the showers in the house, which also feature walls made of completely frameless, freestanding glass.

The use of stone continues into the backyard, where palm trees, boulders and fountain sprays paint a picture of California ease. The massing of native boulders on a shelf that allows them to creep into the pool has become very popular, as has the concept of joining the Jacuzzi to the main pool with an innovative feature, in this case, a small waterfall made from a dam faced with slate.

The Rustic Look

While stone has a certain quality that equates to elegance and upscale living, the material also has the ability to create a more casual home style. For homeowners who are seeking a relaxing retreat, there are ways to implement stone in a design to create a more rustic approach.

Some people who are nature lovers want to bring the serene, soothing atmosphere of the great outdoors into their homes. To achieve this rustic look, rough-faced stones rich in textures, such as fieldstone and slate, are used. Because each region seems to have its own version of these stones—with unique colors and characteristics—they can truly reflect the surrounding environment of the residence.

While fieldstone is often used for foundations and exterior and interior walls, slate is an appropriate choice for patios, walkways and interior flooring. Additionally, both materials are ideal for fireplace surrounds and hearths. Using large, rough-cut pieces of these stones in a fireplace application truly evokes a rustic feeling inside.

Limestone and granite are also options when looking to implement a rustic design. Given a split-faced or bushhammered finish—which gives stone a bumpy, rough texture—these materials can create a natural design style.

A local feel

The owners of a private residence near Spokane, Washington, took advantage of the abundant natural building materials near their location in the Pacific

This residence near Spokane, Washington, connects to the surrounding environment through the use of natural materials. "We tried to keep our materials palette as pure as possible," said designer Dennis Sweeney. "The aesthetic discipline of limiting ourselves to granite, cedar, aluminum and glass produced the simple, sharp, clean contrast that we wanted."

Designer:	**Sun Design, Colville, Washington**
General Contractor:	**Silvey Construction, Spokane, Washington**
Stone Quarrier/Fabricator:	**Yoho Natural Stone Inc., Campbell River, British Columbia, Canada**
Stone Fabricator:	**Big Sky Stone, Hayden Lake, Idaho (oversized slabs)**
Stone Installer:	**Visions Stone Works Ltd., Nanaimo, British Columbia, Canada**
Photos:	**Barry Coon, Commercial Photographers**

After seeing a sample of Glacier Grey granite from a quarry, the owners and their children drove from Spokane to Canada to meet with the principals of the stone quarry to inspect the mine, which sits amid the mountainous wilderness of Vancouver Island. The final decision was to clad the exterior of the residence with 400 tons of the material in a split-faced finish.

Northwest. With its varied terrain of mountains, forests and grasslands, this region offers a unique living environment. Homeowners can live within a natural setting while working in nearby major metropolitan areas. The residence the owners built features an extensive amount of granite from the area.

The house is set in a small draw subdivided by a seasonal stream. Pine, tamarack, and cottonwood trees cover the slopes. The owners, a busy Spokane couple with four children, were very involved in the design, and the setting of the home was a major factor in determining the material selection.

"From the very outset of the design process, we knew we needed a strong, massive base to anchor the house to the hillside in this steep ravine," explains Dennis Sweeney of Sun Design, who designed the home along with his partner, Patrick Gaughan. "We discussed brick and block, and we even investigated acid-etched, tilt-up concrete. While this was going on, the owner was searching the Internet for material, and he discovered this striking pure granite. We knew instantly that we had found our bold base."

The material chosen was Glacier Grey granite, which was quarried and fabricated on Vancouver Island in British Columbia, Canada. In total, four hundred tons of granite were employed for the residence.

But even though the use of granite was discussed from the beginning, it took four months before the owners settled on a stone supplier. An engineer by training, the homeowner played an active role in selecting craftspeople for the four creative skill sets—designer, builder, stone supplier and stonemason.

After initial e-mails and telephone contact with the stone quarrier, Yoho Stone, the company sent the owners and their designer a split-face sample of Glacier Grey, the company's traditional blue-gray coastal granite. A few weeks later, the couple and their family drove to Canada to meet with the principals of Yoho Stone and inspect the quarry, which sits amid the mountainous wilderness of Vancouver Island. The quarry and fabrication plant are located in Campbell River, about five hundred miles northwest of Spokane. The quarry site—one of three owned by the company—is a large boulder field with massive granite blocks strewn about the valley floor below a 7,000-foot mountain peak.

The lower walls of the residence required about 6,000 square feet of exterior stone, which was split on six sides to achieve a 4- to 5-inch-thick bedding. Tiles,

Rough quarry-block faces with sawn backs provide a transition—and climbing wall for the children—linking the site's natural bedrock to the house.

Installer:
    Visions Stone Works Ltd., Nanaimo, British Columbia, Canada

Photos:
    Barry Coon, Commercial Photographers

kitchen and bath slabs, stair treads and other sawn products were all cut from Glacier Grey blocks. This included 24 x 24-inch flamed tiles that were suitable for exterior paving. Some 3,000 square feet of these tiles were specified for both the exterior and interior. Exterior tiles—weighing 110 pounds each—were 2 inches thick and some were mounted on a floating pedestal grid. Interior tiles were 1 inch thick and were honed rather than flamed.

The project required fourteen full truckloads of granite products, which were freighted to Spokane over a period of twelve months. Meanwhile, granite slab material for the kitchen, bath, and an office desk-top were shipped to Idaho for final trim and installation.

The home is anchored with three fireplaces, all done in Glacier Grey and Wild Rose granites. The Wild Rose granite features large pink orthoclase crystals, and it is quarried in the British Columbia interior—not far from Spokane, Washington, but on the Canadian side of the border.

"The fireplace and chimney presented another design opportunity that we could use to pin the house to the hillside with a large vertical element," explains Sweeney. "The steep ravine offers interesting views—from the interior as well as from the roof terraces that result from stepping the house back and up the hillside. The granite pavers and granite-clad terrace walls are ideal no-maintenance choices for these situations.

"We tried to keep our materials palette as pure as possible," the designer continues. "The aesthetic discipline of limiting ourselves to granite, cedar, aluminum, and glass produced the simple, sharp, clean contrast that we wanted."

Above:

The interior flooring of the residence features 24 x 24-inch tiles of Glacier Grey granite with a honed finish.

Right:

Full slabs of Glacier Grey granite were used for the kitchen countertops.

"On the rocks"

The design objective for a vacation home in Heber Springs, Arkansas, was also to tie into the natural surroundings, but with different stone materials. For this project, a local fieldstone was chosen to help achieve the desired aesthetic.

"We do a fair amount of work with fieldstone," says architect Louis Pounders, AIA, co-founder of Williamson Pounders Architects in Memphis, Tennessee. "What we try to do is design structures to be appropriate for their settings. The choice is always driven by the site and its context."

The stone base of this weekend residence in Heber Springs, Arkansas, was intentionally designed to appear as if it grew out of the rock ledge on-site. Dry-stacked stones form a retaining wall and posts at the back of the house.

A local fieldstone was chosen for the exterior façade to reflect the home's rustic setting.

In the main living area of the house, two floor-to-ceiling fireplaces built of fieldstone serve as "bookends" on either end of the room.

Architect:
Williamson Pounders Architects, Memphis, Tennessee
Photos:
Tod Swiecichowski

According to the architects, the logical choice for the Heber Springs residence was fieldstone. "When we first went to look at the property to decide where to put the house, we saw these two huge boulders," states Pounders. "We decided to use those as a key as to where to site the house."

Pounders explains that the owners are a family from Memphis. The 2,800-square-foot house, which is about a three-hour drive from their home, sits on the Little Red River in the Arkansas Hills. The architects decided to perch the new home on a rock ledge overlooking a ravine on the four-acre site.

"It was just natural that the house would evolve from the outcroppings," comments Pounders, adding that the stone base of the residence appears as if it grew out of the site. "There's the main body of the house and a separate garage with a parking court between them. It's sited so that when you drive up to the garage, you can see one of the boulders. It's almost as big as the garage. The other boulder is behind the house. You can't see it until you're inside. It's an enormous piece of rock."

According to the architect, the property is very steep. "We cut a retaining wall around the back of the house," says Pounders. "It's dry-stacked stone. Because the house sits on a sloping site, one side has the porch up in the air sitting on big stone piers. The other side sits on the ground and there is a stone terrace."

The house itself is a pointed shape, remarks Pounders. "The main room is rectangular. It's a tall space with a vaulted ceiling. There are two tall stone fireplaces on each end of the room—like bookends."

In addition to the main residence, there is a 1,000-square-foot screened gazebo with an adjacent fire pit area and dock as well as a 650-square-foot garage. "The design went pretty fast," says the architect. "It took about six months to develop and over a year to build. The stonework is just fantastic."

Combining wood and stone

Also craving a rustic motif for their vacation home were the owners of a residence in Lake Geneva, Wisconsin. They sought to create a casual atmosphere through the use of more subdued materials. And while the choice of Engelmann spruce timber from Canada seemed like an obvious option, the use of marble and travertine was more of a pleasant surprise. By furnishing the stone with a subdued finish, the stone fabricator was able to achieve an informal feel while still using premium materials.

The flooring and vertical surfaces throughout the residence employ a range of stone materials, including Noce and Scabas travertine as well as Rosa Aurora and Rosa Perlino marble. All of the stone was given a Millennium finish, wherein the stone goes through a patented fabricating process that gives it an undulating, subdued appearance similar to tumbled stone but in larger tile formats. The stone flooring in the living room is Noce travertine specified as planking, with pieces measuring 16 inches in width and varying lengths.

"We were building a very casual log-style summer home, and the idea of using marble inside that kind of a home never dawned on us until we saw this product," explains homeowner Robert Forbis, who served as the on-site construction manager for the project. "We had planned on using some antiqued stone in the bathrooms, but when we saw the Millennium product, we changed the entire first floor to that. It absolutely fit the house beautifully."

Forbis explains that although the choice of stone was a consideration from the beginning, there was a concern that it would look too extravagant. "We didn't want something formal-looking and highly polished," he says. "Originally, we had planned on using multicolored green slate throughout the kitchen and foyer, then we learned of this new product. The stone supplier showed us a crate full of colors in that finish, and my wife and I thought it would be perfect. We had spent months going through tile catalogs trying to figure out what to do in the bathrooms, and then we came upon this Millennium-finish stone, and we changed the whole design palette to marble."

Once the selection of the stone was made, crews worked quickly to fabricate the material and get it into place. Approximately 4,000 square feet of stone was specified for the project. "It was the end of May, and we wanted to move in by the end of July," Forbis comments. "The stone supplier really went out of his way to make up the entire order in a week's time, including four custom-made large mosaics. We had

The owners of this Lake Geneva, Wisconsin, residence sought to create a casual atmosphere. The flooring and vertical surfaces throughout the residence employ a range of stone materials, including travertine and marble as well as river rock for several large interior fireplaces (above). Fieldstone was used extensively on the exterior.

Stone Installers: **Hines Masonry, Lake Geneva, Wisconsin (river rock)**
Sheldon Landscape Contractors, Fontana, Wisconsin (Chilton stone)

met him for the first time on May 24, and he shipped the entire order a week later."

Even though the project was in Wisconsin, the installation of the stone was completed by United Stone, a Florida-based firm. "I was having trouble finding a local contractor that could do this type of work the way it needed to be done, so the crew from United Stone came in. The quality of the workmanship was extraordinary. These men really know their stonework."

All of the stone was mud set, and a crack membrane was also installed to ensure longevity for the stonework. In addition to the plank flooring, the home features a variety of innovative stone usages. In the "pheasant" bathroom, the Millennium finish was used throughout. For the shower walls, 12 x 12-inch Scabas travertine tiles were used, while the shower floor is a 3 x 4-foot mosaic. The remainder of the bathroom floor uses 8 x 16-inch travertine pieces as planking. The space also includes a vanity that was made from an antique-replica table. For this feature, smaller Millennium-finished tiles were set on the vanity top, and the sink was dropped into the table.

Another predominant feature of the home was pastel river rock from the Snake River in Montana. Four semitrailers were used to ship the stone from Montana to Wisconsin. The stone was used extensively on the exterior of the home as well as in several large interior fireplaces. Some of the most impressive stonework can be found at the rear of the home. Chilton stone was used for the exterior patio, steps and retaining wall. The material sizes include 2-inch-thick pieces for the patio flooring, 8-inch-thick slabs for the stairs, and 12- to 16-inch-thick slabs for the retaining wall.

This bathroom in the Lake Geneva house includes a vanity made from a replica antique table. For this feature, smaller Millennium-finished tiles were set on the vanity top, and the sink was dropped into the table.

The flooring is comprised of 8 x 16-inch Scabas travertine tiles, which were laid as planking.

Stone Fabricator & Supplier:
Siena Marble & Mosaic, Naples, Florida
Stone Installer:
United Stone, Naples, Florida

Matching existing stone

For an addition to a home in Pennsylvania, a traditional local stone was chosen to match the existing architecture—giving the design a native feel. "The pool and guest wing doubled the size of the house, including extensive slate exterior decking continuing around the pool," says architect Michael Yetterberg of Bower Lewis Thrower Architects in Philadelphia. "The exterior decking and the interior around the pool is all slate. Again, it continued what was already in use around the house. The walls are all Wissahickon schist."

In some areas, such as in the bathroom and guest suite, the homeowners opted for decorative tile, which was available through a supplier of tile products.

Choosing the mason to install the stonework was a key to the success of the job. "There was an Italian mason involved with this who did fabulous work in terms of the sharpness," says Yetterberg. "There are various places where there were oddball angles in the plan for the stonework, and the masons did a fabulous job. The only negative was that we found one stone to form the lintel on the upper fireplace but gave up looking for a stone to form the lintel on the lower fireplace."

For a home in the suburbs of Philadelphia, Pennsylvania, the addition of a pool and guest wing doubled the size of the house. Wissahickon schist, a local stone of traditional use, was employed for the renovation.

Comprising the lintel
on the upper fireplace
in the residence is a
rough-cut slab of stone
that was hand-selected
from the quarry.

Opposite:

Slate was used exten-
sively for the sur-
rounding pool decks.

Architect: **Bower Lewis Thrower
Architects, Philadelphia,
Pennsylvania**
Stone Quarrier: **Media Quarries
(Wissahickon schist)**
Photos: **Don Pearse
Photographers Inc.**

When discussing the design of
the house, Yetterberg
explained that there were various places with oddball angles
in the plan for the stonework.
For applications such as this, it
was critical to have an experienced stone installer. "The
masons did a fabulous job,"
he said.

Old-World Charm

Given the history of natural stone over the centuries, the material has become a logical choice for homeowners seeking an image that recalls the classic architectural styling of years past.

Dubbed the old-world look by many builders and designers, this aesthetic has often been carried through with the use of stone that has been furnished with a patina to mimic the pattern of natural wear over years. Frequently, other appointments in the home—such as classical lighting fixtures, distressed wooden cabinetry or antique furnishings—contribute to this design goal.

A Tuscan flavor

For an upscale home in Tucson, Arizona, a broad variety of stone was employed to achieve a classical Italian look. "They were going with a Tuscany theme," says project contractor Michael Lettera of America Tile West, "trying to get an old-world flavor."

According to Lettera, the homeowners did not want to use carpet, so the design had to be conducive to having tile throughout the 4,600-square-foot residence. "They wanted everything in the house to be a natural product," he comments. "My suggestion in the design phase was to use stone throughout the entire house and vary the colors."

The floors are covered with 24 x 24-inch Oniciata Bruno tiles, which have a

Stone materials play an important role in this old-world style house in the Palm Springs area. From the China Multi Slate roof, down to the rustic Santa Barbara sandstone covering the retaining walls, the stone partners well with the extensive plantings in this backyard.

Owners: **Jack and Vicki Kerns**
Architect: **James Cioffi, Palm Springs, California**
Contractor: **D. W. Johnson Construction, Inc., Palm Springs, California**
Stone Supplier: **Modern Building Materials, Cathedral City, California**
Photo: **Kurt Wahlner**

3/4-inch thickness. This rich travertine was imported from Tivoli, Italy. "We also did a 5-inch baseboard molding throughout the entire house," says Lettera.

In the kitchen, Parana granite slab was used for the countertops. This exotic and colorful polished material imported from India complements the travertine floor. Further enhancing the look of the kitchen is a dramatic hood over the range, which was made from tumbled Scabas travertine from the Tuscany region of Italy. Each piece of Scabas was individually cut to 1 x 4 inches and set in a textured pattern, which displays an occasional lifted stone to create a relief.

The use of Oniciata Bruno travertine extends into the master bath, where the material was all custom-fabricated. "The design for the master bath came about by its sheer size," remarks Lettera. "It's a huge room. I think we figured that we had over 6,000 cut pieces and over 2,500 linear feet of polished edges, which were hand-polished on the job site."

The walls and tub deck of the master bath are custom-cut pieces of Oniciata Bruno—each in a unique size and individually bullnosed and honed on-site to create the old-world look. The vanity tops were fabricated from slabs of the same Italian travertine.

For the Jack-and-Jill bath, a unique pattern was created using 4 x 4-inch tiles of Italian Classic tumbled marble. A shiplap design was used for the tile arrangement to create a dramatic relief. "We wanted to create that old-world

For an upscale home in Tucson, Arizona, a broad variety of stone was employed for a classical Italian look. The home-owners did not want to use carpet at all, so the design had to accommodate tile throughout the 4,600-square-foot residence. The floors are covered with 24 x 24-inch Oniciata Bruno tiles, which have a 3/4-inch thickness. This rich travertine was imported from Tivoli, Italy.

Near right:
Adding another stone to the mix, hand-carved piñon-colored cantera stone ropes surround the mirror and form the angled vanity top in the powder room. The stone, in shades of gray and brown, was imported from Mexico and chosen for its inherent regional characteristics. The various pieces were carved by Mexican artisans, then brought to the job site.

Center right:
Addressing the curved vertical surfaces in this sink area, the design employs 4 x 4-inch tumbled tiles of Oniciata Bruno. The tiles were used for the vanity top and facing as well as the back-splash, wainscot and wall niche. A rough-cut stone sink adds to the overall theme.

Far right:
For the Jack-and-Jill bath, a unique pattern was created with 4 x 4-inch tiles of Italian Classic tumbled marble. A shiplap design was used for the tile arrangement, making a dramatic relief.

Contractor: **America Tile West, Tucson, Arizona**
Stone Supplier: **Arizona Tile, Tucson, Arizona**
Photos: **Brett Drury Architectural Photography, Inc.**

character with the texturing," says Lettera. The 4 x 4-inch format was carried into the guest bath, although Pueblo Stone—a tumbled marble imported from Mexico—was used instead of Italian marble.

Adding another stone to the mix, hand-carved piñon-colored cantera stone ropes surround the mirror and form the angled vanity top in the powder room. The stone, in shades of gray and brown, was imported from Mexico and chosen for its inherent characteristics. According to Lettera, the stone was carved by Mexican artisans and then brought to the job site piece by piece.

In total, it took a little over five months to complete the stone installation, with four masons working six days a week. "There is a lot of warmth and richness in the house," comments Lettera. "Everything is kind of softened and rounded. It has a great feel to it."

Turning back the clock

In her design for a new private residence in the Los Angeles area, Susan Witman of Center Q Interior Design wanted to give the home a classic, aged appearance. "It was a brand-new house that my client had purchased, and we wanted a house that looked a hundred years old or older," Witman says. "We wanted things that would look worn before they were even installed." This philosophy led to the use of antiqued Camargue limestone throughout the interior.

The antiqued limestone was supplied in a variety of formats. In the foyer, the limestone was specified as 16 x 16-inch tiles—set on the diagonal—with a border of 16 x 8-inch tiles. In addition, 4 x 4-inch Nero Marquina tiles were used as an accent. "Camargue was selected first as a material, and then the others were chosen around that," the designer comments. "I know this client really well. She's not afraid of color and detail. The black didn't intimidate her."

In other spaces of the home, such as the living area, the use of antiqued 16 x 16-inch Camargue tiles continues, but the tiles were set square to "accentuate that it was a different area," Witman says. And while Nero Marquina was

Although the owners purchased this Los Angeles residence brand-new, they wanted it to look at least a century old. This design objective was carried out by using antiqued flooring of Camargue limestone in 16 x 16-inch tiles set on the diagonal and accented with 4 x 4-inch tiles of Nero Marquina.

Interior Designer: **Susan Witman, Center Q Interior Design, Ketchum, Idaho**
Stone Supplier: **Walker Zanger, Sylmar, California**

not chosen as a flooring accent in the living room, it was used as a mosaic around the fireplace opening.

In the powder room off the main foyer, the combination of antiqued Camargue and Nero Marquina can again be found, but with a very subtle touch. The 16 x 16-inch Camargue tiles were set on the diagonal, with a banding stripe of $^5/_8$-inch Pietre Romane dots and a single key $^5/_8$-inch Nero Marquina dot where the corners of the tiles meet. "It was a funky, fun detail to use," Witman says.

And even though the limestone was sealed, the weathered look remained. "If you use the correct sealer, I don't think it takes away from the look of the tile," she remarks. "I wouldn't use anything with a gloss or a sheen; anything we use has a matte finish."

By weathering the stone as well as other elements, such as the woodwork in the kitchen, the designer was able to reach the design goal for the home. "The entire residence has a look to it where you have no idea you're looking at something that's just been built," she comments. "I think the materials lent themselves to that type of setting."

Blending with the décor

In choosing the flooring material for their residence in Litchfield, Connecticut, the homeowners wanted something that would complement the artwork within the residence—including faux mural paintings on the walls. And while several different types of stone were used throughout the 12,000-square-foot home, all of the materials were given a tumbled finish to achieve the design objectives.

"The homeowners made the selection of the stone," explains Jean-Claude Minier of Country Flair Tile in Kent, Connecticut, the stone contractor for the project. "They didn't use a designer, so it was me working with them. They wanted an elegant home with some rustic touches to it. They have a lot of artwork on the walls, so it's elegant, but at the same time, it's very artsy."

While tumbled stone was a consideration from the very beginning, the homeowners went through a variety of choices based on color. "Usually, we start with a color and go from there," Minier says.

In the living room/reception area, the tumbled stone was used in a large-

The art of the floor is evident everywhere in this Connecticut home.

Right, above:

In the living room/reception area, there is a field of tumbled 16 x 16-inch yellow travertine tiles with Heliodoro latticework used in a large-format pattern.

Far right, above:

Some of the most innovative stonework is seen at the base of this circular staircase. Tumbled 4 x 4-inch Oro Rosso limestone tiles are set in a spherical pattern, circling a limestone centerpiece.

Right, below:

The kitchen floor employs tumbled Rosa Scabas tiles in a 12 x 12-inch format.

Far right, below:

A combination of tumbled 6 x 6-inch tiles of Café Rosita with 2 x 2-inch black accents is found in the master bedroom.

Stone Supplier:
Walker Zanger, Sylmar, California
Stone Contractor:
Country Flair Tile, Kent, Connecticut
Photos:
Steve Nichols

format pattern, with a field of tumbled 16 x 16-inch yellow travertine tiles with Heliodoro latticework. The kitchen floor employs Rosa Scabas tiles in a 12 x 12-inch format, and the master bedroom and bath features 6 x 6-inch tiles of Café Rosita with 2 x 2-inch black accents.

Some of the most innovative stonework can be found at the base of the circular staircase. In this area, tumbled 4 x 4-inch Oro Rosso limestone tiles are set in a spherical pattern, circling around a limestone centerpiece.

Redefining a classic residence

In restructuring a Westchester County, New York, residence that was originally built in 1916, the new design called for a change in the building's floor plan but relied upon antiqued stone to maintain the classic theme of the home. The previous owners of the home had resided there for forty years without doing any renovation work, and the new owners sought to completely update the residence while respecting its classical styling.

In one area, several rooms were gutted and made into a combination master bath/dressing area/closet. On the bathroom floor, the field material is comprised of tumbled tiles of Botticino marble from Italy in sizes of 4 x 4, 8 x 8 and 12 x 12 inches. A custom-made border consists of $^3/_4$ x $^3/_4$- and 2 x 2-inch pieces of tumbled Perlino Rosato, Giallo Reale and Botticino marble. A custom center medallion in the bathroom

space was created using these three stones in many different sizes. The medallion and border reflect the same outlines of the Adam-style ceiling.

For the bathroom walls, Botticino was again the predominant marble in various sizes, with Perlino Rosato rail and bar moldings. The shower seat and shelves were fabricated from honed $3/4$-inch-thick Botticino Semi-Classico slabs, which were also used for the tub deck and stairs.

A complete renovation was also executed on the first level of the home, where several smaller rooms were combined to form the kitchen. The floor in this area consists of limestone, with a custom border pattern of tumbled Noce travertine, limestone and Botticino marble. As an added feature, the same stones were also set within the millwork.

Meanwhile, the countertops are $1^{1}/4$-inch-thick slabs of Golden Juparana granite, quarried in Brazil. The same granite was also used for windowsills and for the top of an antique serving buffet located at the entrance to the eating area.

The kitchen area leads to a dining room/winter garden, with the limestone floors continuing throughout. As in the kitchen, the limestone field tiles are highlighted with a border pattern but arranged in a design that fits the scale of the room.

In restructuring a Westchester County, New York, residence originally built in 1916, the new design called for a change in the building's floor plan but relied upon antiqued stone to maintain the classic theme of the home.

Several rooms were gutted and made into a combination master bath/dressing area/ closet. A custom center medallion in the bathroom space was created using the same stones in many different sizes. The medallion and border reflect the outlines of the Adam-style ceiling.

A complete renovation was also executed on the first level of the home, where several smaller rooms were combined to form the kitchen. In this space, a limestone floor is complemented by a custom border pattern of tumbled Noce travertine, limestone and Botticino marble. As an added feature, the same stones are set within the millwork.

Stone Supplier:
    Walker Zanger,
    Sylmar, California

Reclaiming history

While natural stone with an antiqued finish can be used to create an aged look in a home, there is another option that lends itself to true authenticity. Although not a booming trend yet, the concept of using salvaged (reclaimed) pieces of stone, mostly extracted from classical homes in Europe, is slowly growing in popularity. When the budget permits, using reclaimed tiles is sure to further enhance an old-world or rustic motif.

Given the broad range of stone usage throughout history, the choice of reclaimed stone can offer homeowners the same flexibility as if they were standard stone products. The material can be cut into smaller tiles such as 4 x 4 inches or employed as large-format tiles. Additionally, homeowners have used stone in a random floor pattern, mirroring some of the timeless floor patterns used in Europe centuries ago.

Because of the age of reclaimed stone, homeowners won't have the concern of wear patterns, which aren't uncommon with marble and limestone applications.

Facing:
Varying from typical floor designs, hexagonal-shaped pieces of French Antique terra-cotta were employed in this kitchen. The multi-colored material brightens up the area and serves as a contrast to the dark cabinetry.

For the bathroom on the left, smaller 4 x 4-inch floor tiles of Giallo Split antique biblical stone complement the wall pattern, which is made of tiny mosaic pieces.
The wall and tub surround on the right is comprised of Lansen Antique terra-cotta. The color and gentle patterning of the pieces conjure a warm inviting atmosphere in the space, and create a rustic feel in the room.

Stone Supplier for all: **Ann Sacks, Portland, Oregon**

The dull patina finish also provides a safe, slip-resistant surface. For these reasons, reclaimed stone can work well in bathrooms and outdoor applications, including patios, pool decks, driveways and walkways.

However, given the one-of-a-kind nature of this type of product, homeowners need to consider the fact that colors and sizes are not guaranteed with reclaimed stone. In many cases, this material has aged for more than a hundred years, and the range in shades can vary drastically. Also, these pieces tend to be thicker (more than 3 cm) than standard stone tiles (1 or 2 cm). Therefore, it is important to hire an installer who is familiar with stone materials of this thickness.

Even though homeowners may face some inconsistencies when using reclaimed stone, they may gain another dimension to their residential design. Rich with history, the reclaimed stone can add to the home's unique character.

Facing:

In addition to interior design, reclaimed stone also adds an attractive touch to exterior applications. Employing Sonoma pavers for this patio terrace helped to create an old-world feel while also tying the residence to its natural surroundings.

A new trend on the rise in residential design is using reclaimed stone, which in many cases has been salvaged from homes in Europe. In this foyer, large-format biblical stone tiles were laid in a random floor pattern.

A driving force

Before designing the residence of NASCAR auto-racing legend Junior Johnson and his wife, Lisa, designer Leo Dowell went on a fact-finding mission with the couple, examining the homes of the rich and famous throughout the country. The result of that mission is a palatial estate in Ronda, North Carolina, that utilizes a substantial amount of natural stone to create a flavor of colonial Mexico.

"Lisa Johnson had been given my name, and she called to tell me about the 10,000-square-foot home she and her husband were planning," Dowell recalls. "Then she mentioned her husband's name, and I knew exactly who he was."

In conceiving a design for the home, Dowell showed the couple "what all the movie stars are doing" with their homes. "We traveled all over the country—mostly in their planes—and they were open to suggestions on what they thought would look good," he says. "Lisa wanted to be educated on how to pick things and how to put things together and we made decisions really fast."

One of the premier design elements was Nube limestone from Mexico, employed in honed 16 x 16 x ¹/₂-inch tiles. "I thought he would want something country, but he's traveled all over the world and he was open to things like limestone and wrought iron," Dowell comments. "He didn't want anything run-of-the-mill."

The designer explains that although the residence was located on a cattle ranch in northern North Carolina, the intention was to create a very distinctive character. "That's why we used a lot of natural materials," he says. In addition to the limestone, a tumbled marble inlay was designed within the limestone at the entrance to the master bathroom, intended to look like an area rug. The mirrors and sconces for the residence were made in Mexico, and all of the cabinetry was drawn and crafted in Dowell's own workshop. Additionally, two different artists came in to paint the walls and the ceiling. The walls were faux-finished in stone

With a floor of honed Nube limestone from Mexico and a tumbled marble inlay, the North Carolina residence of NASCAR legend Junior Johnson and his wife, Lisa, was designed with a colonial Mexican theme. The walls were faux-finished in stone and brick, while the ceilings depict a cloud-filled sky.

Owners: **Junior and Lisa Johnson**
Designer: **Leo Dowell Interiors, Charlotte, North Carolina**
Stone Quarrier: **Mayabtun, Yucatán, Mexico**
Stone Supplier: **The Dean Agency Intl., Ltd., Charlotte, North Carolina**
Contractor: **Al Richards**
Photo: **© Robert Starling Photography**

In addition to the flooring, the Jacuzzi surround and vanity top are made from Mexican limestone. The tiles were 16 x 16 x ½ inches with a honed finish.

Photo:
Pat Shanklin

and brick, while the *trompe l'oeil* ceilings depict a cloud-filled sky.

One amenity that the Johnsons thought to add in the bathroom was a heating system, which was installed beneath the limestone flooring. Also, the Jacuzzi was hooked up to a special telephone line so it can be turned on by remote—preparing itself for when the Johnsons arrive home.

Upon completion, the house was so impressive that the producers of the television series *Baywatch* used it for their program. "They were doing an episode about a race-car driver, and they're using this house in the series," Dowell explains. "It's like the opening to the old television show *Dallas*, where they will show an aerial view. The producers interviewed Junior Johnson and his wife and decided to change the character because they didn't think he would live this extravagantly."

Additionally, the home has been the focus of two TV specials on ESPN, and certain rooms have appeared in ten national magazines. In crediting the success of the project, Dowell cited the owners as a key factor. "Junior Johnson was one of the best clients I worked with because he was open to suggestions and ideas. That's how he got where he is," he remarks. "He finds people who are good at something, and he lets them do their thing. He wanted it to be right and one of a kind. One of the things Johnson liked about the project was that people often said, 'It can't be done.' But that's the name of the game these days—to do what cannot be done."

The limestone combines with the painted elements and window seats to carry the colonial Mexican flavor throughout the home.

Photo:
© Robert Starling Photography

When architect James Cioffi was interviewed to design this new home for Jack and Vicki Kerns, the first thing he was asked was, "Are you a romantic?" Romantic charm was the watch phrase through the entire house, starting out with the gate leading up to the front door. Jack Kerns runs a landscaping business, so, naturally, the plantings and flowers share the stage with the house, which is covered with a cultured stone called Santa Barbara Rustic sandstone. It was broken into small pieces and affixed to the structure. The moldings around the doors and windows are cement that has been hard troweled. The entrance court is paved with Utah Blonde in random flats. The stone musical angels atop the entry newel posts were initially Christmastime decorations but are now on permanent duty.

Owners:	Jack and Vicki Kerns
Architect:	James Cioffi, Palm Springs, California
Landscape Architect:	Jack Kerns
Contractor:	D. W. Johnson Construction, Inc., Palm Springs, California
Landscape Installation:	Hort Tech, Palm Springs, California
Stone Supplier:	Modern Building Materials, Cathedral City, California
Photos:	Kurt Wahlner

The interior of the Kerns house has something of the feeling of being in a castle out in the countryside, from the living room to the kitchen. All the floors are of travertine marble, while the fireplace in the living room was constructed of preexisting concrete parts ordered from a catalog.

The kitchen features counters made of Giallo Vereziano granite, which also forms a backsplash/shelf above the stove. The stove hood is flanked by the Santa Barbara Rustic sandstone.

The backyard has an upper level which completely encircles a swimming pool, which is on a lower level from the house.

Below, from left to right:

A small fireplace outside the master bedroom is covered with Coco pebbles and Coco flats. A view along the top terrace running along the house (all of the walkways on this level are Utah Blonde flats). The fountain facing the swimming pool, with its pre-cast Gianninni basins set in a background of 6 x 6-inch China Multi slate (the same as is used on the roof of the house). A view of the pool with the terraced gardens surrounding it (the pavers around the pool itself are Antique Cobble in a cream-colored blend).

149

The focus of the backyard is the pool, with its waterfall fountain made of Natural Brown Round boulders from Desert Rock Supply. Each one had to be carefully placed in position and allowed to settle before the next course was laid. There is a Jacuzzi at the top of the waterfall, as well as a waterslide, lined with small Carrara marble mosaics.

Above:

To one side of the pool is this peaceful pergola. The uprights rest on footers of the same Utah Blonde flats that comprise the walkways.

151

Stone-Look Materials

With the increased popularity of natural stone, producers of man-made materials have capitalized on design trends by offering products that mirror the look of natural stone. Perhaps the most noteworthy products of this type are "stone-look" ceramic tiles and man-made countertops such as DuPont Corian as well as DuPont Zodiaq.

"Stone-look" tiles

While the concept of creating ceramic tiles to mimic natural stone is certainly not a new one, manufacturers of these products—in the United States and abroad—are focusing on this trend more than ever before. Ceramic tiles are being designed to replicate all varieties and finishes of natural stone, from the look of polished marble to weathered limestone and even water-worn river stones.

Ceramic tiles are being produced with the random depressions and shadings of natural stone, and manufacturers have been able to create tiles that feature a dominant color with touches of varying accents, mirroring the unique aesthetic qualities of natural stone. Moreover, these tiles are being produced with rectified and beveled edges that can effectively duplicate the look of natural stone in a finished installation.

For consumers, the use of ceramic tile over natural stone offers a number of

Ceramic tile manufacturers have been striving to create stone-look products that mimic the natural qualities of the material. These ceramic tiles—dubbed Terra Forte, or "strong land"—are designed to mirror the look of weathered stone flooring. They are available with complementary pieces for the wall base.

Tile Manufacturer: **Interceramic, USA, Garland, Texas**

potential advantages, starting with cost. For the most part, the price of stone-look ceramic tiles is lower than that of their natural-stone counterparts.

There are also practical benefits to installing and utilizing a product made in a factory as opposed to one extracted from the earth. Typically, ceramic tiles have no variations in thickness or dimensions, while poorly fabricated stone tiles may require special attention during the installation—such as a "mud bed" application (a thick mortar bed allowing for variance in tile thickness) or wider grout joints—to accommodate slight differences in tile sizes.

Ceramic tile has also been used to simulate the look of highly polished marbles, as shown by the Expressions series. Decorative field tiles and listel borders complete the look.

Light marbleizing and soft neutral colors define this series of tile, which is called "Cabos." It is complemented with a listel depicting a leaf pattern, as well as a bullnosed ceramic molding at the upper wall.

Tile Manufacturer: **Interceramic, USA, Garland, Texas**

Although advances in manufacturing "stone-look" ceramic tiles have been made over the years, they still maintain a manufactured look, with each tile in a product line having consistencies with the next tile in the same line. This is not a characteristic of natural stone, but it may be considered an advantage for home-owners seeking a consistent, homogeneous aesthetic. If you want the look of natural stone with added uniformity and only part of the expense, this is a viable way to go.

The Escapades line of ceramic tile features a natural-stone look in six earthy colors, with an individual stone border.

An old-stone look with subtle detailing is provided by the Kennesaw line, featuring three rich colors and a variety of size options.

Tile Manufacturer: **American Florim, Clarksville, Tennessee**

Solid-surface countertops

The overwhelming man-made competitor to natural stone countertops is DuPont Corian. A blend of natural materials and pure acrylic polymer, Corian falls into the classification of "solid surfaces," which was created by DuPont more than thirty years ago.

Corian is manufactured by DuPont in the form of sheets and sinks. The sheets are precut in specific lengths at the factories and then shipped to a worldwide network of distributors. Like natural granite countertops, Corian solid surfaces are engineered to be smooth and nonporous. As a result, they will not promote the growth of mold, mildew, or bacteria. And the nonporous nature of the product ensures that liquids and stains cannot penetrate it, making it relatively easy to clean and maintain. Also consistent with natural stone, Corian is non-toxic, chemically nonreactive and hypoallergenic, with virtually no off-gassing at normal room temperatures, in accordance with building codes and other local restrictions.

Although Corian and similar man-made countertop products such as Avonite and Transolid feature many of natural stone's practical benefits, the aesthetic differences between man-made countertops and natural-stone countertops are even more pronounced than the differences between natural-stone tiles and ceramic imitations. Depending on the personal preferences of the homeowner, this can be a benefit or a disadvantage.

While solid-surface materials can offer a more homogeneous look, granite creates that one-of-a-kind appearance, varying even within a single countertop space. From a fabrication standpoint, installing granite countertops throughout a single kitchen space typically requires specifying multiple slabs, which means there will be seams that have to be grouted and maintained. Since a solid surface can be thermoformed, it can be used seamlessly to achieve both traditional and nontraditional designs. A typical sheet of Corian can be transformed into a dramatic curved stairway or a sculpted piece of furniture. Additionally, solid-surface countertops can be shaped to create a coved backsplash and offer the option of submounting, top-mounting, or joining a sink of the same material without a seam. Transolid, a solid-surface manufacturer that specializes in sinks and bowls, offers countertops with a sink and coved backsplash in one piece for a bathroom vanity. Granite sinks are also available but cannot be installed without a seam, and a granite backsplash is available only with a straight edge. "With the technology and installation methods of granite, the seam is a small price to pay for the beauty of it, and it is usually not noticed," explains Fred

An attempt to combine ergonomics and luxury can be found in the "Le Cob Bath," designed by Joseph Licciardi in DuPont Corian Cameo White. This freestanding bath features a curved profile and glass sides, allowing water to trickle over the body from one end and cascade like a waterfall into a concealed drainage tray. The concept behind the bath is to fully submerge the body along a supportive form, allowing it to be soothed by the natural flow of water.

Manufacturer: **DuPont Surfaces, Wilmington, Delaware**

Hueston of NTC Enterprises, a stone-preservation firm based in Longwood, Florida. "Your eyes do not go to the seams."

Routine daily care and maintenance of solid surfaces is similar to that of natural stone. Soapy water or ammonia-based cleaners will remove most dirt and stains from all types of finishes. Because Corian and comparable solid-surface products are solid all the way through, minor damage—including scratches, general or chemical stains, scorches or burns, and minor impact marks—can be repaired on-site with a light abrasive cleanser and a product such as a 3M Scotch-Brite pad. (See the chapter "Maintenance in Mind" for detailed information on maintenance and repair.)

Engineered quartz surfacing

Recently, manufacturers have introduced quartz engineered surfacing to the marketplace as a way of bridging the gap between man-made materials and natural stone products. One of the firms at the forefront of this

Contrasting with the brightly colored cabinetry in this kitchen space, the counters are made with DuPont Zodiaq quartz surfacing in Vortex Black.

Manufacturer:
DuPont Surfaces, Wilmington, Delaware

movement has been DuPont, which introduced Zodiaq quartz surfacing. Made almost entirely of pure quartz crystals, the product offers a sleek uniform look with high durability and scratch-resistant properties. The product is manufactured in color patterns inspired by nature, including earth tones of beige and green as well as other tones not attainable naturally, such as vibrant blue and red hues. In residential environments, the product can be used for kitchen and bathroom countertops as well as backsplashes, wet bars, tub decks and showers. The material is available in large sheets—measuring as large as 52 inches, with thicknesses of 2 and 3 cm. The material can be machined, sandblasted and inlaid, with a wide variety of edge treatments available.

While DuPont has been one of the most visible suppliers of engineered quartz surfacing, they are not the only manufacturer of this product. Outside the United States, manufacturers such as Caesarstone in Israel; Cosentino, S.A., in Spain; and Santa Margherita and Agglo Baghin in Italy are also producing engineered quartz products, and they are actively marketing them in the American marketplace (contact information for all of these companies can be found in the "Resources" section).

Comparative costs of installing stone-look products vs. natural stone

In choosing building products, homeowners need to remember that they will not only be paying for the products themselves but for the entire installation of those products. So when choosing between two flooring materials such as natural stone tiles or ceramic tiles designed to look like natural stone, the cost goes beyond the price of the tiles themselves. It includes such installation products as mortar and grout, and, of course, the labor charges from the tile setter. Generally, the products used for installing natural stone are the same as those used for installing ceramic tile. (There are exceptions, however, which is why a contractor with natural-stone experience is strongly advised.)

While it is important to make sure that the contractor who installs a natural-stone tile floor has experience with the material, the overall cost should not be higher than the cost for installing ceramic tile. A tile setter who is experienced with natural stone will be aware of the special needs of certain stone materials, but the time required to install a stone-tile floor should remain on par with the

In this bathroom design, a sleek contemporary look was achieved with DuPont Zodiaq quartz surfacing. The design includes Celestial Blue for the tub deck, countertop and vanity, with Cloud White for the wall and tub surround.

Manufacturer:
DuPont Surfaces, Wilmington, Delaware

time required for a ceramic floor.

In the area of kitchen countertops and vanities, depending on the type of stone or solid surface material chosen, the price will fluctuate, and solid surfaces can actually end up being more costly than natural stone. "There are varying degrees and ranges of both materials, and some of the higher-end solid-surface materials can be more expensive than granite," explains Hueston. "Sometimes they are equal in price, and other times a solid surface is cheaper than granite." For example, if a solid color is chosen for a solid-surface material, its cost will be less expensive than one with a pattern. Another factor that contributes to the cost of both materials is the amount of fabrication involved. "The price of granite is usually controlled or dictated by the amount of fabrication necessary," says Hueston. "If a bullnosed edge or undermount sink is needed, it requires more fabrication and is more expensive." The same is true with solid surfacing. If a homeowner is seeking a coved backsplash rather than a standard backsplash, or if a different color is inlaid into the edge of a solid-surface counter, there is more labor involved, and this will raise the end price.

Though the installation of a solid-surface countertop is easier than granite, this does not have a large effect on the price. "A solid surface is a little easier to install because it is lightweight and would not take as many individuals to install it as are needed with granite," says Hueston. "But for the most part they are about equal as far as installation costs."

After clearing away any false information and considering the pros, cons, and various options of both granite and solid-surface countertops, the final choice is ultimately up to the owner. More often than not, the choice of using a man-made material over natural stone is made for aesthetic reasons rather than price issues.

Opposite:

The pastel look of natural quartzite is evoked in the Mythos line of ceramic tile. This variety, named Vesuvius Ash, has a consistent bluish-gray tone not available in natural stone.

Tile Manufacturer:
Daltile, Dallas, Texas

Maintenance in Mind

A common misconception regarding natural stone is that it is a completely indestructible, maintenance-free product. While it is true that natural stone will wear better than almost all man-made building products, there are care and maintenance issues that should be kept in mind before and after installing stone in a home.

When specifying natural stone for a home, it is important to bear in mind that not all stones are suitable for all applications. There are many external factors that can affect the appearance of a stone installation, and it is important to understand these factors before the stone is specified.

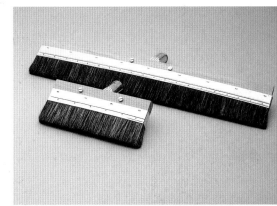

Exterior stone selection

When using stone for an outside application, the most obvious concern is weathering. In harsher climates, where freeze/thaw cycles can severely damage certain stone materials, choosing the right stone is critical. Even in a mild climate, it is important to choose a stone—and a stone finish—that will stand up to the elements.

From a practical point of view, stones that have a textured finish have proven to be the least affected by the elements. Because they already have a

With the help of chemical sealers, the long-term durability of a stone installation is greatly enhanced. Sealers invisibly protect stone, forming a barrier to repel stains and water damage. Many of today's sealers on the market can be easily applied by homeowners with simple brushes as shown above. Reapplication of a sealer will be necessary over time, although the standard life of a sealer application is more than a year, depending upon surface traffic.

Photos courtesy of: **HMK Stone Care System, San Francisco, California**

Stone isn't maintenance-free, but some stone selections have lesser requirements than others. At a minimum, exterior stone should be protected from water sprinklers to maintain its beauty longer.

Left: Quartzite veneer on the Ken and Sandra Walker home. *Right:* West Desert Stone and aged brick are some of the blended elements on the Bruce and Edna Albertson home.

General Contractor (both homes):
**Cameo Homes,
Salt Lake City, Utah**
Stone Suppliers:
Western States Stone Supply (quartzite)
Stone Mason:
Western States Stone Masonry, Inc. (quartzite),

patina on the surface, stones with a cleft face or other texturing will typically not change dramatically in appearance—even in harsh climates. On the other hand, highly polished marbles can lose their luster in the long term, and certain varieties can even begin to spall and flake when exposed to the elements. Additionally, stone materials with a high degree of porosity will absorb a higher proportion of water than denser stones, which can cause cracking during the freezing/thawing cycles in colder climates.

To avoid problems with stone on an exterior installation, ask the stone supplier where you can see examples of how a stone performs over time in similar applications. Understand that while aesthetics are the first reason for choosing a stone, the technical qualities of a material are also key factors in determining which is the right stone for a home.

Interior stone selection

For interior stone applications, two of the most common problems for natural stone are excessive wear and staining. Keeping the wear of natural stone to a minimum is a simple matter of selecting the proper material for the proper application. Natural-stone flooring in an entry foyer or stone floor tiles in front of a kitchen or bathroom sink are subject to an extremely high level of foot traffic, and choosing the wrong stone can result in obvious and unsightly patterns on the surface. For this reason, it is important to rely on an experienced stone supplier who can recommend materials that are appropriate for their final application—based on a successful history of use for that specific purpose.

It is also important to consider that even within a single category of natural stone—whether it is marble, granite, limestone, or another type of stone—the technical characteristics can vary greatly. For example, French limestone is much denser and has a higher level of resistance to wear than most other types of limestone, making it more suitable for high-traffic flooring applications.

Unfortunately, because there are countless varieties of natural stone, there are few generalities that can be made about the material and its suitability for various applications. Typically, granites have the densest, most durable composition, while some limestone and travertine varieties are among the softer stones. However, these are basic rule-of-thumb concepts. When choosing a stone for an application—from kitchen countertops to exterior driveway cobblestones—it is best to choose a stone that has already been used successfully for that specific function.

A durable flooring material such as slate for heavily traveled floors will offer greater long-term benefits than virtually any man-made material. In this design, Broughton Moor slate from England was used for the flooring, countertops and the center island, providing an ideal surface for all types of kitchen work.

Stone Supplier: **Burlington Natstone, Plano, Texas**

Mixing materials

Another factor to consider when using natural stone is how it will perform alongside other materials, and even how it will perform when installed along with other types of stone. Creative designers have combined natural stone with glass, metal, ceramics, and wood to achieve a desired aesthetic. However, these alternative materials will weather quite differently than natural stone, and the various maintenance and weathering issues should be considered before an installation is completed. Experienced stone suppliers should be able to inform homeowners on how a specific stone product will weather when used alongside alternate materials in traditional combinations—including those using ceramic, glass, or even wood—and they should be able to explain exactly what maintenance concerns will arise for each design.

Additionally, design schemes where multiple stones are juxtaposed against one another—such as a granite countertop with a marble tile backsplash—may also have different maintenance procedures within a single space. Again, a professional with experience in the stone industry should be able to explain the specific issues with these design combinations.

The maintenance of natural stone should be considered prior to installation, particularly when it is combined with other materials. In this residential project, Pierre Du Nile stone is combined with natural wood for the flooring. The two products have very different maintenance requirements, and all cleaning products should be specific for the product treated.

Stone Supplier:
Creative Tile Marketing, Miami, Florida

Kitchen environments commonly combine natural stone with ceramic tile, and there are specific care considerations for each material. In this design, tumbled natural-stone varieties in sand and walnut for the walls are combined with ceramic-tile flooring.

Stone Supplier: **Daltile, Dallas, Texas**

Stone sealers

Even when the right stone is chosen for an application, it is still subject to some degree of staining. Simply stated, natural stone stains because it is porous in nature (the level of porosity depends on the type of stone). Certain fluids and pollutants can enter these pores and become embedded below the surface of the stone. When the surface of a stone is honed or textured, these pores are even more pronounced, making it more susceptible to staining.

One way to offset this possibility is by treating the stone with a sealer soon after it is installed. With the help of chemical sealers, the long-term durability of a stone installation is greatly enhanced. Today, homeowners can select from a much larger variety of stones than in the past, knowing that the stones that were avoided in the past due to their hard-to-clean nature can now be made stain-resistant with the help of these products. Sealers protect stone invisibly, forming a barrier to repel stains and water damage.

Just as there are countless maintenance products for materials such as wood, ceramic tile and carpeting, there are also dozens and dozens of sealers for natural stone. Because every sealer has a specific effect on stone, choosing the right sealer greatly depends on what the homeowner desires in the final outcome. It is important to point out that certain sealers can actually change the look of a stone surface.

In addition to how a sealer will affect the appearance of a stone, other factors to keep in mind include the stone's hardness and porosity (information that should be provided by the stone supplier) as well as where it will be installed. Interior applications of natural stone will be subjected to obvious types of staining, based on which room they are located in. Most likely, kitchen environments will require an additional resistance to cooking grease and oils, while an entry foyer will be subject to dirt and wear from heavy foot traffic.

There are many ways that sealers can be classified, but one of the most important distinctions is between surface sealers, which tend to be topical in nature, and impregnating sealers, which penetrate deeper into the body of the stone. Surface sealers tend to be water-based and offer a barrier to repel stains and water damage. They are recommended for use on highly porous stones, as they fill the crevasses of materials such as limestone, slate, adoquin, travertine, shellstone, sandstone and flagstone.

Depending on the type of stone, the pores can be a place for dirt to accumulate, making the stone more and more unattractive over time. Using a surface sealer will help reduce the need for ongoing care and maintenance. The standard life of a surface-sealer application is one year, and depending upon surface traffic, reapplication of the sealer will be necessary over time.

In addition to providing surface protection, some sealers can enhance the

In kitchen areas, natural stone can be subject to staining, particularly from elements such as red wine, olive oil and cooking grease. By pre-sealing natural stone in a kitchen space, these factors are minimized. In this room, African slate is used for the floor and vertical surfaces, while limestone forms the countertop.

Stone Supplier:
   **Walker Zanger,
   Sylmar, California**

look of a stone. Homeowners can use sealers that add a matte finish or even a high-gloss sheen to the surface of a stone. As with any product of this type, however, it is strongly advised that you test the product in an inconspicuous area (or on a sample piece of stone, if possible) to see the final effect a sealer will have on a stone surface.

Performing quite differently from surface sealers, impregnating stone sealers penetrate into the body of the stone and have a natural look with no sheen. Impregnators that can repel both water-based and oil-based contaminants are recommended for any application where the stone will be subjected to a broad variety of stains, such as kitchen environments. A quality impregnator will create a barrier resistant to surface absorption, increase the static coefficient of friction (slip-resistance factor), make the surface harder, and allow vapor permeability without changing the natural characteristics of the stone or the grout.

The longevity of an impregnating sealer will vary depending on the surface texture, type of stone, where it is located, and what type of wear the surface is exposed to. Typically, reapplication is recommended every three to ten years for residential floors, and every one to three years for countertops.

A sealer should be either 0 or 1 on the toxicity level (which rates products on a scale of 0 to 4), which is no more than household laundry detergent. For kitchen countertops, the sealer should be approved for use in food preparation areas. Most sealers should be simple to apply and reapply using a spray pump, clean towels, or a mop. The surface should look wet to the eye, and then the excess should be removed after a few minutes.

Overall, the maintenance concerns for natural stone are not excessive when compared to other high-end materials such as natural wood, fabrics or metals. By conducting simple day-to-day and preventive maintenance, such as sealing stones in applications that require added protection, a natural stone installation will truly last a lifetime.

The maintenance of natural stone—and preventive maintenance such as sealing—also plays a factor in a bathroom environment. In this design, the Porto Beige limestone vanity top and surround must be sealed to ensure its longevity.

Stone Supplier: **Walker Zanger, Sylmar, California**

Surface Sealers

Advantages

- Typically economical, with a relatively low price for initial application
- Easy to apply
- Provide a coating on the stone that will absorb more of the overall wear
- Can provide luster

Disadvantages

- Since the product is softer than the stone itself, it can be scratched and scuffed, requiring frequent buffing or reapplication
- Can build up over time, producing an unnatural look on the stone
- Require more frequent stripping and reapplication, which can damage the stone
- Could inhibit the "breathability" of stone, causing moisture to be trapped below the surface

Impregnating Sealers

Advantages

- Typically do not change the appearance of stone
- Do not require frequent applications
- Can typically repel water-based and oil-based stains
- Can possibly add slip-resistance

Disadvantages

- Higher in price than surface sealers
- Could be less effective below grade due to hydrostatic pressure

Designers

Alison Whittaker Design
P.O. Box 320366
Los Gatos, CA 95032
408.395.5388
408.395.7348 fax

Arch-Interiors Design Group, Inc.
275 South Robertson Blvd
Beverly Hills, CA 90211
310.652.7600
310.652.7602 fax
www.archinteriors.com

Bower Lewis Thrower Architects
1216 Arch Street
Philadelphia, PA 19107-2835
215.563.3900
215.563.3036 fax
www.blta.com

Barbara H. Karpf Interiors, Inc.
1160 Park Avenue
New York, NY 10128
212.722.6449
212.369.5765 fax

Calder Interiors
1365 York Avenue
New York, NY 10021
212.861.9055
212.249.2131 fax

Center Q Interior Design
323 Lewis Street #J
Ketchum, ID 83340
208.726.3639
208.726.3640 fax

CONstruct Architects
3750 Minnehaha Avenue
Minneapolis, MN 55406
612.724.9877
612.724.1394 fax

Dave Prest, Architect
74020 Allesandro, Suite C
Palm Desert, CA 92260
760.779.5393

Drysdale Design Associates
1733 Connecticut Avenue NW
Washington, DC 20009
202.588.0700

Gene Zettle Interiors
22 South Oakland
Pasadena, CA 91101
626.792.2844

Gullans & Brooks Associates Inc.
87 Main Street
New Canaan, CT 06840
203.966.8440
203.966.3191 fax

James Cioffi, Architect
2121 East Tahquitz #3
Palm Springs, CA 92262
760.325.1557

Kearney & O'Banion Design
1401 Illinois Street
San Francisco, CA 94107
415.824.1069
415.824.6530 fax

Kevin McKenna Architects
Box 722
Columbia, MD 21045
410.381.5817
410.381.0929 fax

Lee H. Skolnick Architecture +
Design Partnership
7 West 22nd Street
New York, NY 10010
212.989.2624
212.727.1702 fax
www.skolnick.com

Leo Dowell Interiors
501 East Morehead Street, Ste 2
Charlotte, NC 28202
704.334.3817

Robert Orr & Associates
Architecture & Gardens
441 Chapel Street
New Haven, CT 06511
203.777.3387
203.776.5684 fax

Romanza Architectural Interiors
2900 North Orange Avenue
Orlando, FL 32804
407.228.0997
407.228.0977 fax

SRM Design Group, Inc.
55 East Main Street
Holmdel, NJ 07733
732.332.0851
732.975.9844 fax

Sun Design
107 North Main Street
Colville, WA 99114-2305
509.684.3244

William Miller Design
P.O. Box 11966
Palm Desert, CA 92255-1966
760.836.9199

Resources

Williamson Pounders Architects
245 Wagner Place, Ste M100
Memphis, TN 38103
901.527.4433
901.527.4478 fax

Stone Suppliers/Contractors

Adera Natural Stone Supply Ltd.
4736 Byrne Road
Burnaby, BC V5J 3H7
Canada
604.436.0204
604.436.0555 fax

Agglo Baghin S.p.A.
Via Callalta 24/A 31039
Riese Pio X TV, Italy
+39.0423.755339
+39.0423.755340 fax
www.agglobaghin.it
Supplier of engineered stone

American Tile West, Inc.
1985 West Paseo Cuenca
Tuscon, AZ 85704
520.797.8120
520.797.7130 fax

Ancor Granite Tile Inc.
435 Port Royal West
Montreal, PQ H3L 2C3
Canada
514.385.9366
514.382.3533 fax
www.ancor.ca

Ann Sacks
8120 NE 33rd Drive
Portland, OR 97211
503.280.9701

503.280.9710 fax
www.annsacks.com
Stores nationwide

Arizona Tile
7248 South Harl Avenue
Tempe, AZ 85283
480.893.9393
480.897.2935 fax
www.arizonatile.com

Bedford Stone
P.O. Box 475
Bedford, NY 10507
914.666.6404
914.666.2526 fax

Brent Miller Stone
120 North 300 West
American Fork, UT 84003
801.763.5658
www.millerstone.com

Burlington Natstone Inc.
2701-C West 15th Street, Ste 505
Plano, TX 75075-7595
972.985.9182
972.612.0847 fax
www.burlingtonstone.co.uk
Specializes in a variety of English slate

Caesarstone
7315 Fulton Avenue
North Hollywood, CA 91605
800.666.8201 inside CA
818.255.4785 outside CA
818.255.4797 fax
www.caesarstoneus.com
Supplier of engineered stone

Cameo Homes
9035 South Canyon Gate Circle
Sandy, Utah 84093
801.942.8780
ryan_quinton@hotmail.com

Ciot Imports Ltd.
9151 St. Laurent
Montreal, PQ H2N 1N2
Canada
514.382.5180
514.382.5990 fax

C. L. Martineau Homes, Inc.
1464 East Ridgeline Drive
Suite 200
Ogden, UT 84405
801.475.4555
clmhomes@msn.com

Connecticut Stone Supplies
138 Woodmont Road
Milford, CT 06460
203.882.1000
203.882.0771 fax

Cosentino S.A.
P.O. Box 1
Macael-Almeria 04867
Spain
34.950.444175
34.950.444226 fax
Supplier of engineered stone

Country Floors
15 East 16th Street
New York, NY 10003
212.627.8300
212.627.7742 fax
www.countryfloors.com
Supplier of reclaimed antique stone as well as other materials

Dean Agency International, Ltd.
2100 Forest Drive East
Charlotte, NC 28211-2164
704.364.2552
www.aaow.com/mayabtun

Delaware Quarries
6603 Route 202
P.O. Box 778
New Hope, PA 18938
215.862.1670
215.862.1685 fax

DuPont Corian
Barley Mill Plaza 12
P.O. Box 80012
Wilmington, DE 19880-0012
800.4.CORIAN
800.426.7426
302.892.1927 fax
www.corian.com

DuPont Zodiaq
Barley Mill Plaza 12
P.O. Box 80012
Wilmington, DE 19880-0012
877.229.3935
302.892.1927 fax
www.zodiaq.com

D. W. Johnson Construction, Inc.
1445 Sunrise Way, Ste 203
Palm Springs, CA 92262
760.416.1144

Eagle Marble and Granite
3035 North Coolidge Street
Los Angeles, CA 90039
323.664.4857

Echeguren Slate, Inc.
1495 Illinois Street
San Francisco, CA 94107
415.206.9443
800.992.0701
415.206.9353 fax
www.echeguren.com

Elizabeth Street Gardens
1176 – 2nd Avenue
New York, NY 10021
212.644.6969

Foxx Homes
73061 Fred Waring Drive
Palm Desert, CA 92260
760.568.5773
www.foxxhomes.com

Grani Décor Tiles Inc.
1040 Bussiere Street
St. Sebastien, PQ G0Y 1M0
Canada
819.652.2361
819.652.2360 fax
www.grani-decor.com
www.polycor.com

Granite & Marble by Malavé
150 Industrial Avenue
Greensboro, NC 27406
336.273.0223
336.273.0669 fax

Haifa Marble
2949 – 2nd Avenue North
Lake Worth, FL 33461
561.641.4911
561.641.8763 fax
www.haifainc.com

Hastings Tile
30 Commercial Street
Freeport, NY 11520
516.379.3500
800.351.0038
516.379.0570 fax
www.hastingstilebath.com

Hort Tech
P.O. Box 3284
Palm Desert, CA 92261
760.360.9000

IGM—International Granite &
Marble
2038 – 83rd Street
North Bergen, NJ 07047
201.869.5200
800 IGM-CORP
201 869-9403 fax
www.igmcorp@igmcorp.com

Jensen Stone
Talmage, UT 84073
801.518.9790

Kirkstone Quarries Ltd.
Skelwith Bridge, Ambleside
Cumbria, LA 22 9NN
England
44.15394.33296
44.15394.34006 fax
www.kirkstone.com
Supplier of English slate

Les Granits Montval, Div. Groupe
Granitcon Inc.
935 Rue Lippmann
Laval, PQ H7S 1G3
Canada
514.382.6017
450.975.7746 fax

L & T Construction
P.O. Box 1999
Orem, UT 84059
L-Tconstruction.com

Marmol Export U.S.A.
3500 NW 79th Avenue
Miami, FL 33122
305.592.1181
305.592.5490 fax
www.marmol.com

Modern Building Materials
825 Grand Avenue
San Marcos, CA 92069
760.591.4570

Morneo Tile
68625 Perez Road
Cathedral City, CA 92234
760.321.1210

National Stone Drafting, Inc.
1873 South Bellaire Street, Ste 935
Denver, CO 80222
303.691.9987

New Mexico Travertine
P.O. Box 439
Belen, NM 87002
800.962.7253

Paris Ceramics
150 East 58th Street, 7th Floor
New York, NY 10155
212.644.2782
212.644.2785 fax
www.parisceramics.com
*Supplier of reclaimed antique stone
as well as other materials*

Pierrexpert
5810 Place Turcot
Montreal, PQ H4C 1W3
Canada
514.932.9266
514.932.2072 fax
www.pierrexpert.com

Quadra Stone Co. Ltd.
1275 – 75th Avenue
Vancouver, BC V6P 3G4
Canada
604.266.5341
604.266.5441 fax
www.quadrastone.com

Quantum Stone International
124 Arnold Crescent
Richmond Hill, ON L4C 3R8
Canada
905.770.7117
800.446.3085
905.770.2545 fax
www.quantumstone.com

Santa Margherita S.p.A.
Via del Marmo 1098
37020 Volargne
Verona, Italy
390.45.6835888
390.45.6835800 fax
www.santamargherita.net
Supplier of engineered stone

Siena Marble & Mosaic
3693 Domestic Avenue
Naples, FL 34104
941.435.7875
941.435.9942 fax

Southland Stone USA, Inc.
12804 Raymer Street
North Hollywood, CA 91605
818.503.1500
800.778.2730
818.503.1501 fax
www.southlandstone.com
Specializes in multicolored Indian slate and vibrant colored sandstone

Stasio Construction, Inc.
57 Golf Lane
Ridgefield, CT 08677
203.431.3946

Stone-Tec, Inc.
2929 West Kingsley
Garland, TX 75041
972.278.4477
972.840.6148 fax

Traditional Cut Stone Ltd.
48 Lavender Road
Toronto, ON M6N 2B7
Canada
416.652.8434
416.652.1591 fax
www.traditionalcutstone.com

United Stone
2259 Drade Center Way
Naples, FL 34109
941.597.7773
941.597.0009 fax

Vetter Stone Co.
P.O. Box 38
Kasota, MN 56050
507.345.4568
507.345.4777 fax
Specializes in Minnesota limestone

Walker Zanger, Inc.
13190 Telfair Avenue
Sylmar, CA 91342
818.504.0235
818.833.0846 fax
www.walkerzanger.com
Offers various product lines of tumbled marble, limestone and travertine as well as numerous shades of other natural stones. Also has a broad range of mosaic borders and medallions

Western States Stone Masonry, Inc.
Western States Stone Supply
981 East Canyon Creek Drive
Bountiful, UT 84010
801.725.9037

World Wide Stone Corp.
15275 N. 83rd Place
Scottsdale, AZ 85260
602.438.1001
602.438.6888 fax
www.durangostone.com
Specializes in a variety of Mexican limestone, travertine and marble

Below and Overleaf:
Architectural details of the Rob Potter home, Farmington, Utah

General Contractor: **Chris Martineau Homes, Inc., Ogden, Utah**
Stone: **Indiana Limestone**
Brick Mason: **Dave Jones Masonry, Mt. Green, Utah**
Stone Supplier: **New Mexico Travertine, Inc.**
Photographer: **Kurt Wahlner**